BOOK ONE: 5 Expert Sys Navigate the Stock Marke

BOOK ONE: 5 Expert Systems to Navigate the Stock Market ...1

Introduction 17

Chapter 1 - What You Should Know About Day Trading 18

    The Day Trader...18

    Your Trading Strategy 20

    Analysing Trading Systems 22

    Selecting Your Market...22

    Selecting Your Time Frame 24

    Selecting A Trading Style..24

    Defining Entry Points 25

    Defining Exit Points 25

Chapter 2 – Trend Following: Moving Averages 27

    Historical Evidence...27

    Defining Entry Points 28

    Defining Exit Points 28

    Setting Up The System 28

Chapter 3 – Trend Following: Cross-Over of Moving Averages 31

    Historical Evidence...31

    Defining Entry Points 31

    Defining Exit Points 32

Setting up the System 32

Chapter 4 – Trend Following: Turtle Trading **34**

Historical Evidence 34

Defining Entry Points 34

Defining Exit Points 35

Setting up the System 36

Chapter 5 – Counter-Trend Following: Williams %R **37**

Historical Evidence 37

Defining Entry Points 37

Defining Exit Points 38

Setting Up The System 38

Chapter 6 – Counter-Trend Following: Relative Strength Index **40**

Historical Evidence 40

Defining Entry Points 41

Defining Exit Points 41

Setting Up The System 42

Chapter 7 – The Secrets to Day Trading Success **43**

Conclusion **46**

What are Cognitive Biases? **57**

Chapter 1 - Stubbornness **59**

Anchoring Bias 59

    Case Study 59

    Your Learning Curve 60

Confirmation Bias 61
    Case Study 61
    Your Learning Curve 61

Post Purchase Rationalism 62
    Case Study 62
    Your Learning Curve 62

Chapter 2 - Fear 63

Loss Aversion Bias 63
    Case Study 63
    Your Learning Curve 63

Recency Bias 64
    Case Study 64
    Your Learning Curve 64

Inaction Inertia 66
    Case Study 66
    Your Learning Curve 66

Chapter 3 - Greed 67

Hyperbolic Discounting Bias 67
    Case Study 67
    Your Learning Curve 67

Chapter 4 - Confidence 69

Illusion of Control (Outcome Bias) 69
    Case Study 69

    Your Learning Curve 70

Hindsight Bias 70
    Case Study 70
    Your Learning Curve 70

Bias Blind Spot 71
    Case Study 71
    Your Learning Curve 71

Chapter 5 – Affect Heuristics 72

Bandwagon Bias 74
    Case Study 74
    Your Learning Curve 74

Ambiguity Effect 75
    Case Study 75
    Your Learning Curve 75

Attribution Bias (Illusory Correlation) 76
    Case Study 76
    Your Learning Curve 76

Social Proof Bias (closely linked to Bandwagon Bias) 77
    Case Study 77
    Your Learning Curve 79

Contrast Bias (Decoy Effect) 80
    Case Study 80
    Your Learning Curve 80

Monte Carlo Fallacy (Gambler's Fallacy) 81
Case Study 81
Your Learning Curve 81

Clustering Bias 82
Case Study 82
Your Learning Curve 82

Authority Bias 83
Case Study 83
Your Learning Curve 83

Hot Hand Bias 84
Case Study 84
Your Learning Curve 84

Martingale Bias 85
Case Study 85
Your Learning Curve 85

Deformation Professionelle Bias 86
Case Study 86
Your Learning Curve 86

Conclusion 87

Glossary of Terms 88

Introduction 100

Chapter 1 - Learning the Basics 101
The Forex Market 101

Getting Started on Forex Trading 103
    Placing an Order 104
Training for Success 105
    Trading Platforms 106

Chapter 2 - Understanding Technicalities 109

The Principal Currencies 109
Forces that Drive the Foreign Exchange Market 111
    Gross Domestic Product 111
    Current Events 111
    Industrial Production Report of the nation 111
    Consumer Price Index 113
    Retail Sales Report 113
How to Understand and Predict Price Movements 113
    Short-term predictions 114
    Long-term predictions 115

Chapter 3 - Forex Trading Systems 117

Simple Moving Average 117
Moving Average Convergence Divergence 121
RSI – Relative Strength Index 123

Chapter 4 - Secrets to Becoming a Successful Forex Trader .. 128

Characteristics of Successful Investors and Traders 128

Chapter 5 - Glossary of Terms 131

Conclusion 133

5 Expert Systems to Navigate the Stock Market
BOOK ONE

Leigh Vernon

Text Copyright © [Leigh Vernon]

All rights reserved. No part of this guide may be reproduced in any form without permission in writing from the publisher except in the case of brief quotations embodied in critical articles or reviews.

Legal & Disclaimer

The information contained in this book and its contents is not designed to replace or take the place of any form of medical or professional advice; and is not meant to replace the need for independent medical, financial, legal or other professional advice or services, as may be required. The content and information in this book has been provided for educational and entertainment purposes only.

The content and information contained in this book has been compiled from sources deemed reliable, and it is accurate to the best of the Author's knowledge, information and belief. However, the Author cannot guarantee its accuracy and validity and cannot be held liable for any errors and/or omissions. Further, changes are periodically made to this book as and when needed. Where appropriate and/or necessary, you must consult a professional (including but not limited to your doctor, attorney, financial advisor or such other professional advisor) before using any of the suggested remedies, techniques, or information in this book.

Upon using the contents and information contained in this book, you agree to hold harmless the Author from and against any damages, costs, and expenses, including any legal fees potentially resulting from the application of any of the information provided by this book. This disclaimer applies to any loss, damages or injury caused by the use and application, whether directly or indirectly, of any advice or information presented, whether for breach of contract, tort, negligence, personal injury, criminal intent, or under any other cause of action.

You agree to accept all risks of using the information presented inside this book.

You agree that by continuing to read this book, where appropriate and/or necessary, you shall consult a professional (including but not limited to your doctor, attorney, or financial advisor or such other advisor as needed) before using any of the suggested remedies, techniques, or information in this book.

Table of Contents

BOOK ONE: 5 Expert Systems to Navigate the Stock Market ...1

Introduction 17

Chapter 1 - What You Should Know About Day Trading 18
- The Day Trader 18
- Your Trading Strategy 20
- Analysing Trading Systems 22
- Selecting Your Market 22
- Selecting Your Time Frame 24
- Selecting A Trading Style 24
- Defining Entry Points 25
- Defining Exit Points 25

Chapter 2 – Trend Following: Moving Averages 27
- Historical Evidence 27
- Defining Entry Points 28
- Defining Exit Points 28
- Setting Up The System 28

Chapter 3 – Trend Following: Cross-Over of Moving Averages
.... 31
- Historical Evidence 31
- Defining Entry Points 31
- Defining Exit Points 32
- Setting up the System 32

Chapter 4 – Trend Following: Turtle Trading 34

Historical Evidence 34

Defining Entry Points 34

Defining Exit Points 35

Setting up the System 36

Chapter 5 – Counter-Trend Following: Williams %R 37

Historical Evidence 37

Defining Entry Points 37

Defining Exit Points 38

Setting Up The System 38

Chapter 6 – Counter-Trend Following: Relative Strength Index 40

Historical Evidence 40

Defining Entry Points 41

Defining Exit Points 41

Setting Up The System 42

Chapter 7 – The Secrets to Day Trading Success 43

Conclusion 46

What are Cognitive Biases? 57

Chapter 1 - Stubbornness 59

Anchoring Bias 59

   Case Study 59

   Your Learning Curve 60

Confirmation Bias 61

   Case Study 61

Your Learning Curve 61

Post Purchase Rationalism 62

   Case Study 62

   Your Learning Curve 62

Chapter 2 - Fear 63

Loss Aversion Bias 63

   Case Study 63

   Your Learning Curve 63

Recency Bias 64

   Case Study 64

   Your Learning Curve 64

Inaction Inertia 66

   Case Study 66

   Your Learning Curve 66

Chapter 3 - Greed 67

Hyperbolic Discounting Bias 67

   Case Study 67

   Your Learning Curve 67

Chapter 4 - Confidence 69

Illusion of Control (Outcome Bias) 69

   Case Study 69

   Your Learning Curve 70

Hindsight Bias 70

  Case Study 70

  Your Learning Curve 70

 Bias Blind Spot 71

  Case Study 71

  Your Learning Curve 71

Chapter 5 – Affect Heuristics 72

 Bandwagon Bias 74

  Case Study 74

  Your Learning Curve 74

 Ambiguity Effect 75

  Case Study 75

  Your Learning Curve 75

 Attribution Bias (Illusory Correlation) 76

  Case Study 76

  Your Learning Curve 76

 Social Proof Bias (closely linked to Bandwagon Bias) 77

  Case Study 77

  Your Learning Curve 79

 Contrast Bias (Decoy Effect) 80

  Case Study 80

  Your Learning Curve 80

 Monte Carlo Fallacy (Gambler's Fallacy) 81

  Case Study 81

Your Learning Curve 81

Clustering Bias 82

  Case Study 82

  Your Learning Curve 82

Authority Bias 83

  Case Study 83

  Your Learning Curve 83

Hot Hand Bias 84

  Case Study 84

  Your Learning Curve 84

Martingale Bias 85

  Case Study 85

  Your Learning Curve 85

Deformation Professionelle Bias 86

  Case Study 86

  Your Learning Curve 86

Conclusion 87

Glossary of Terms 88

Introduction 100

Chapter 1 - Learning the Basics 101

  The Forex Market 101

  Getting Started on Forex Trading 103

    Placing an Order 104

Training for Success 105
    Trading Platforms 106

Chapter 2 - Understanding Technicalities 109

The Principal Currencies 109

Forces that Drive the Foreign Exchange Market 111
    Gross Domestic Product 111
    Current Events 111
    Industrial Production Report of the nation 111
    Consumer Price Index 113
    Retail Sales Report 113

How to Understand and Predict Price Movements 113
    Short-term predictions 114
    Long-term predictions 115

Chapter 3 - Forex Trading Systems 117

Simple Moving Average 117

Moving Average Convergence Divergence 121

RSI – Relative Strength Index 123

Chapter 4 - Secrets to Becoming a Successful Forex Trader .. 128

Characteristics of Successful Investors and Traders 128

Chapter 5 - Glossary of Terms 131

Conclusion 133

Introduction

The day trading business is as predictable as weather. There are highs and lows that occur within hours, even minutes and seconds from each other. Day trading is essentially defined as the buying and selling of a security – a negotiable financial instrument that holds some type of monetary value. What makes it even more interesting and challenging is that the trade occurs in the same day, in a span of hours, minutes, or even seconds. Most day tradings can occur in the foreign exchange rate and stock market. Day traders contribute to keeping the market running efficiently by providing liquidity and arbitrage.

However, it is important to note that this book does not guarantee that you can make giant profits or provide sure-win methods in trading. Instead, it is assumed that you have already engaged in day trading activities, and are on the hunt for proven strategies to polish your existing ones, or to replace them. As a day trader, all the rules you have learned about finding good stocks over the years won't matter. Day trading is a completely different game with its own set of rules, but if you know what you are doing you will be able to fine-tune strategies that work best for you.

This book will help guide you to become the day trader you want to be. It may not happen automatically and all at once, but making money is possible if you put in the time, effort, commitment, and dedication it demands.

Chapter 1 - What You Should Know About Day Trading

The Day Trader

A day trader can be two things: a risk manager and a hunter of volatility. Simply put, the job of a day trader is one who buys shares of a certain stock and sells it within a number of minutes or hours in order to gain a profit. This is why day traders look for volatility in such a short period of time. This is influenced by any of these three things: companies that have just released news, reported earnings, or other reasons that increase public interest. All these things influence how a day trader chooses to enter and exit a particular stock or share.

There are two types of day traders. The first one is a professional who works for large financial institutions. Some will say that this is the best place for you to start because you will most likely have a mentor – and several other professionals – guiding you on how to do the tricks of the trade. You will have access to tools and the latest technology to help you analyse your strategies. With this arrangement, you will be paid a basic salary and occasionally a bonus. Perhaps the best take-away with this is that you won't be using your own money to trade, saving you the risk of time and money, while enjoying employee benefits.

The second type is called the individual trader. Armed with the ability to understand technical analysis and how the market works in a thorough sense, they trade for themselves. They also have a large quantity of money to invest in, mainly because the gains will be miniscule if you only invest a small amount. These are the people who have learned to define their own trading style through experience.

What makes a good day trader? Many theories surround this topic, with a number of conflicting and opposing views. Even if two individuals start with the same capital, the same trading platform, and the same trading systems with the same entry and exit points, the results can still be different. So what the key difference that sets them apart? It's not about intelligence, inherent talent, or even dedication and focus. Both people want to succeed, so why does one enjoy a profit while the other one suffers loss?

In a book by American psychologist Dr. Van Tharp, he discussed the role of psychology in trading – and it's much more significant than you think. In a pie chart he calls the "Ingredients of Trading", he divides three aspects – system, management, and psychology. System accounted for 10% of the pie, with Management next on the list at 30%. Interestingly, psychology clocked in at 60% - the biggest part of the pie that accounts for the top influencer and difference in the styles of day traders. But what exactly is this psychology he was referring to, and how can it help us become better day traders?

In a nutshell, psychology refers to your emotions, feelings, thoughts, and actions that affect your investment decisions. Day trading in the stock market makes it possible for you to gain profit and lessen risk, but emotions often play a huge influence on how you react and handle different situations. Take for example the day trader who is prone to react emotionally, and in the end makes various wrong decisions. He keeps holding on to a losing position, with the belief that it will turn out to be a winner – someday. This classic mistake has a name to it and it is called loss aversion. It is the tendency for people to defer likely gains by holding on tight and avoiding losses. Even with the market spiralling downward, loss aversion keeps traders from letting go and cutting off losses. What is even more interesting is that traders of this nature usually display signs of other irrational behaviour. An example of this is attributing success to exceptional trading skills and losses to bad timing and bad luck. Without controlling your emotions, you will lose money very quickly in the markets. This is because you are reacting on impulse and holding on to strong beliefs that can be damaging to your portfolio.

If emotions play a large part in determining whether you will succeed or fail in day trading, how then can we change our psychology? How can we shift our focus and learn to manage and keep our emotions under control? How can we keep a cool and rational head in order to be more receptive to the fluctuations in the market?

The answer lies in discipline. A successful day trader never rests on his own laurels. He knows that he's never reached the peak of his skills and abilities just yet, despite past successes. He makes conscious and deliberate choices when making decisions, until this ability develops muscle memory. Discipline then, can be trained, when practiced daily and deliberately.

Another important skill in order to be a successful day trader is to develop your own set of trading rules. This should guide you on when to enter or exit a stock. Over time, and after accumulating years of experience and trying out different strategies, you will soon reach a point where you find a comfortable and effective way to trade. Once you find the sweet spot that works for you, stick to it, improve it, and implement it. Lastly, keep your emotions in check at all times. Having self-control can make you immune to the highs and lows of trading, and help keep your cool through the downturn, panic, or euphoria that occurs during day trading. Learn to accept losses with grace and move on to the next one.

Over time, you will learn that you will inevitably lose without discipline. You may have the right skills but when you allow greed and fear to start taking control over your decisions, you will not succeed. The most important thing to ask yourself here is whether you have the commitment to remain disciplined, as discipline can be learned.

Your Trading Strategy

At 11:10 am, a day trader might buy 1,000 shares on McDonald's stocks just when prices begin to increase due to the release of good news. The day trader then decides to sell the stock at 11:20 am when the stocks climb up by $1 per share. With this, he can easily make $1,000 in just 10 minutes. How does he do it?

A great day trader accepts that each trade he makes has its own level of risk, and he adheres to a specific set of rules set for that trade. This is called trading strategy. It includes rules in defining when to enter and to exit, based on certain conditions, trade triggers, timeframe, management of money and financials, and other relevant and useful information. It also includes historical data based on previous trends and performance in order to project future performance.

When a trading strategy is properly executed, it can give you a mathematical expectation for how to determine if a certain trade is really profitable or not. While trading strategies aren't free from limitations, it does provide a risk-adjusted return, which may or may not guarantee success on your part. They are a great way to avoid financial biases and help to secure consistent results over a long period of time.

The success rate of day traders is estimated to be only around 10%, with a whopping 90% losing money. And top of this, only 1% really make serious profit. By definition, if you are buying, then there must be someone selling. With this analogy, then there must be someone making money, while the other one loses money. This is why trading strategies are the backbone of any day trader. Without a properly designed one, you will be heading into battle without a helmet on.

While the importance of trading strategies cannot be over-emphasised, the downside is that they are difficult to develop. It's easy to become reliant on one strategy, but it does not ensure that you will get the same positive result at all times. While there are some methodologies with a ready set of rules handed down to us, there will come a time when you must devise your very own. Your system has to reflect who you are. But despite the differences, and seemingly opposing sets of rules for different day trading strategies, only one thing is common – the system needs to be systematic. Regardless of how unique your circumstances are, putting in place a defined system can strap you in for the long-term. When designing your own system, ask yourself of the following questions:

- Is my system designed for capital growth or cash flow?
- Am I trading part-time or full-time?
- How much money can I afford to lose?
- What percentage of annual rate am I aiming for?

Analysing Trading Systems

There are systems that buy on strength and sell on weakness, while others do the exact opposite. Some may make their millions through momentum trading; others are more comfortable as value investors. Despite the fact that there are many methods, there are countless ways to gain profit as well.

If a trading strategy works in a system, then there has to be several parts that constitute to it as a whole. Typically, a trading system has the following:

- Selecting your market
- Selecting your time frame
- Selecting a trading style
- Defining entry points
- Defining exit points
- Evaluation
- Improving your trading strategy

In order to understand different trading systems, we need to take a look at these parts individually.

Selecting Your Market

Financial instruments in recent times have allowed private investors to have a variety of choices in trading. In addition, these have also been enhanced by virtue of the introduction of electronic contracts that make it easier to access shares and stocks. For example, you can invest in real estate investment fund without even owning a property. These days, traders have the option to trade anything amid everything available to them.

The four main markets include stocks, Forex, futures, and stock options. As only stocks and Forex are primarily used in day trading, only these two will be discussed.

The stock market can be a public or private market that is used for the trading of a company stock on an agreed price. When a company makes itself available on the stock market, it is given a value by investors, wherein the value of the company is divided into what we know as shares. You, as a day trader, can have the capacity to buy and sell these shares in return, making you a shareholder of a company for a certain time. The value of the company can increase or decrease, bringing the value of your bought shares along with it. When the company makes a profit, you may receive some of that profit in the form of dividends. This profit is divided amongst everyone who owns shares in the company. While stocks markets usually have good volatility and liquidity, the requirements for initial capital are usually high.

The second market in focus is Forex, which is the abbreviation of the term Foreign Exchange. Just like any other form of trading, it follows the basic rule of buying when the market is going up, and selling when it is going down. The only difference is that with Forex trading, the day trader buys and sells currencies. In simpler terms, it's the exchange of currency at an agreed upon rate for another currency. All currencies are automatic participants in this trade, but just as there are blue chips stocks, there are also currencies that stand out as more powerful ones than all others. The top five are the US dollar, the Japanese Yen, the British Pound, the Swiss Franc, and the European Union Euro. Take note that you will always need to trade currencies in pairs, buying one currency while simultaneously selling another. Because it requires only a small amount of capital and less emotional investment, Forex trading can be a great start to polish your trading skills to prepare you for higher and more difficult markets.

Selecting Your Time Frame

Day trading time frames are set only within a particular day, but intraday timeframes can range as low as 1 minute or as high as 60 minutes, perhaps even more. With smaller timeframes, the average profit is usually low, but in exchange, you get higher trading opportunities. The opposite occurs when you trade in a larger timeframe – the average profit will be bigger, but there will be fewer chances to trade. If you're just starting out, it is better to try trading in smaller timeframes at first. This way, you can prevent over-leveraging your account and have minimal associated risk. The only problem with too short timeframes is that you can encounter a lot of distractions and short manipulated moves that you can mistake for an emerging trend. This is why the ideal timeframe is 15 minutes. It is small enough for intraday moves, and large enough to establish trends and reduce "noise".

Selecting A Trading Style

Trading systems can generally be broken down into technical strategies and fundamental strategies. Both can be tested on accuracy because they rely on quantifiable information. The main difference is that with technical strategies, the day trader relies on generating technical signals from technical indicators, while fundamental strategies consider fundamental factors into account. For example, a technical trading strategy may involve the use of a moving-average cross-over; in the fundamental arena, the investor looks at other specific criteria like revenue or growth to evaluate his opportunity.

By definition, fundamental stock analysis requires the day trader to take a close examination of financial statements of the company. The day trader will then most likely estimate whether the stocks are undervalued or overvalued, by virtue of the company's current financial strength, current management skills, future growth, and profitability prospects. Annual and quarterly reports are given importance as well as any news or rumours about the company.

On the other hand, the premise of technical analysis lies in the understanding that patterns tend to repeat themselves and tend to follow a certain direction. It involves the study of stocks with the use of charts, graphs, support and resistance levels, trendlines, and other mathematical tools which will help the day trader establish and predict future movements in order to identify opportunities.

Defining Entry Points

Because the market is constantly moving, you need to be able to identify entry points and make decisions at the speed of lightning. It all sounds complicated at first, but the skills needed for this can be learned. When deciding when to enter, practice identifying the entry rules of your chosen strategy. If you know your selected approach very well, learn its own rules. Make sure you understand the market condition and select the best strategy that is most suited for that trend. Don't worry about exit points just yet – focus on getting an entry first, as stipulated by the rules of your chosen system.

Defining Exit Points

Now you have come to the most important crux of trading. Here are three points you need to know in order to exit effectively:

- *Stop loss*

This is defined as the limit used to prevent the loss form being too damaging when the trade goes against you. If you don't apply stop losses in your trading, chances are you will be losing a lot of your capital. The trick here is for you to make a set of rules and stick to those rules no matter what. Know when the right time is for you to cut a losing position before entering a trade. Once you've entered a trade, place a stop at once. This ensures you won't be losing all of your money. Remember, profit is far more important than pride. Admit defeat when your trade backfires and exit in order to lessen the opportunity cost, and use the remaining freed capital elsewhere to fight back.

- *Profit taking exits*

Once you begin seeing profits in your trade, it can be very tempting to sit back and ride the wave as much as you can before making an exit. Human beings are by nature greedy, and this can often contribute to their downfall. Instead of taking huge profits on a single trade, try to take smaller profits consistently instead. The easiest to do this would be to specify a target profit and exit when it is achieved.

- *Time stops*

While the first two exit strategies require you to set stop losses and profit exit points, exiting on these pre-determined values, Time Stops allow you to decide on your exit only after you entered a trade. This strategy requires your full attention to the emerging trends in your trade, and this is where technical analysis can be of great help. An example of a good time stop is three times the time-frame you're using. If you are using charts of 15-minute timeframes, consider abandoning the trade if you have not reached your target within 45 minutes. Your entry might be wrong if nothing happens after a certain time.

Now that you've familiarized yourself with the different aspects of trading, we can now take a look at some day trading systems you can use in the subsequent chapters.

Chapter 2 – Trend Following: Moving Averages

Historical Evidence

Moving averages are among the most popular and simplest methods of trading. Simply put, it is done by calculating the mathematical mean of a given set of values. In other words, a set of numbers - say the closing prices within a 10-day period – are added up together and divided by the number of values in that set. The resulting number is the moving average, not just a regular average or mean due to the nature of trading. Since old data must be dropped from the set and new values must come and replace them, this value is dynamic as opposed to static. Once these points are plotted onto a chart, they are connected to create a moving average line.

Figure 1
Source: https://www.investopedia.com/markets/

Take a look at this simple moving average chart above. The blue line represents a moving average of 50 days. You will notice that the trend has been continuously moving lower since 2007, reaching its average in January 2008 as it begins to dip.

Defining Entry Points

Using the same chart, we can determine the entry point for this trading system. When the chart crosses below a moving average, it suggests that the asset price will likely continue to fall. This can be seen as a trade signal for entry for those traders who believe they can profit from a decline in stock prices. Conversely, when the price crosses above the moving average, the asset price may be ready to increase. This can also signal another entry point for the trader who purchases securities in order to sell them later at a higher price.

Defining Exit Points

Exit strategies typically involve setting up prior stop-loss limits to avoid the emotional response of being too confident that the trend will continue and missing out on other opportunities. A common exit strategy for moving averages is exiting on strength. The day trader will need to look for a signal of strength towards the direction of his first initial entry and make the exit. This way, the trader can lock in his profits before the rest of the market jump on the bandwagon, which may prompt a possible reversal. Some of the indicators you can use to determine exit points are pivot target, percentage ATR, and oscillator extremes. These advanced technical terms and strategies need to be studied separately in order to further understand when the best time to exit would be.

Setting Up The System

Now, how does one determine which is the best market to trade in? By using a concept called relative strength, you will be able to identify which is the best at any given time. Take a look at the charts below:

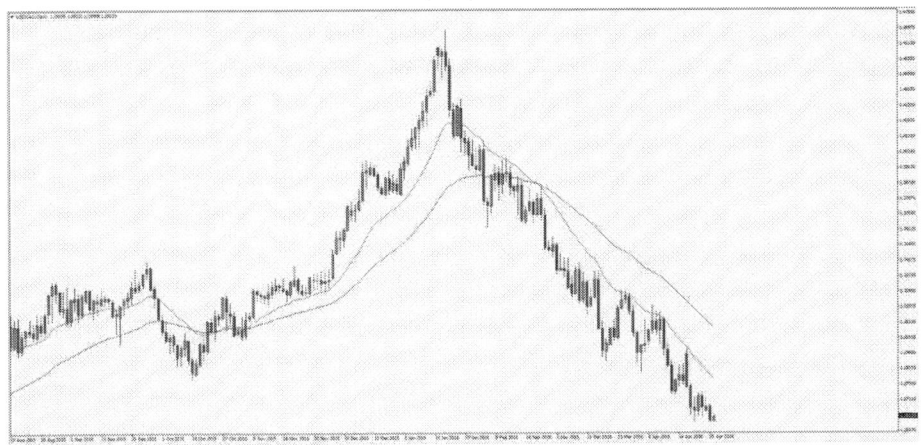

Figure 2
Source: https://my-pull-zone-tradingwithrayne.netdna-ssl.com/wp-content/uploads/2016/06/relative-strength-usdcad.jpg

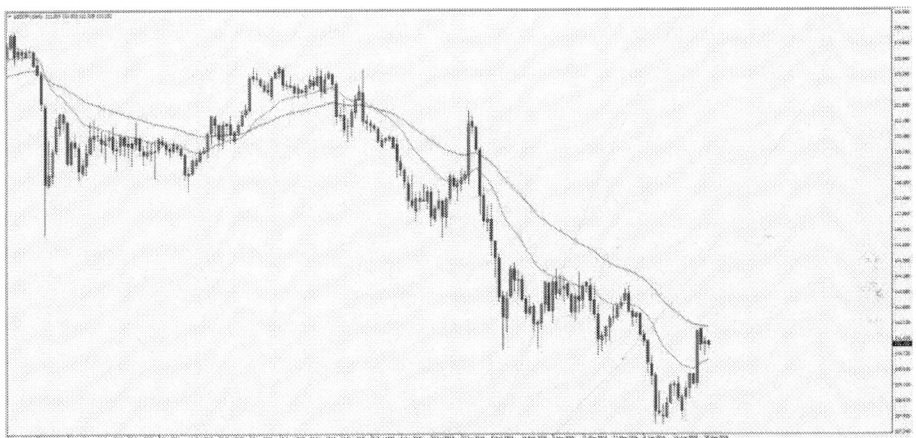

Figure 3
Source: https://my-pull-zone-tradingwithrayne.netdna-ssl.com/wp-content/uploads/2016/06/relative-strength-usdjpy.jpg

Compare the steepness of each chart's moving average. The steeper it is, the stronger/weaker the market will be. In this case, you would want to short the market in the first chart instead of the second chart where the market is relatively weaker.

Here is an example of how to use Moving Averages in trading:

- If the 200-day moving average is increasing exponentially and the price is above the line, then there is an uptrend.
- If you are using the 20-50 day period of moving averages, wait for the two-test dynamic support.
- If this price test is supported twice, make your entry on the third try.
- Place a stop loss of 2 ATR if long, or exit when you're wrong.
- If the price moves according to your favour, then take profits when the candle closes beyond 50 exponential moving averages.

Below is a sample on how to trade using this moving averages system:

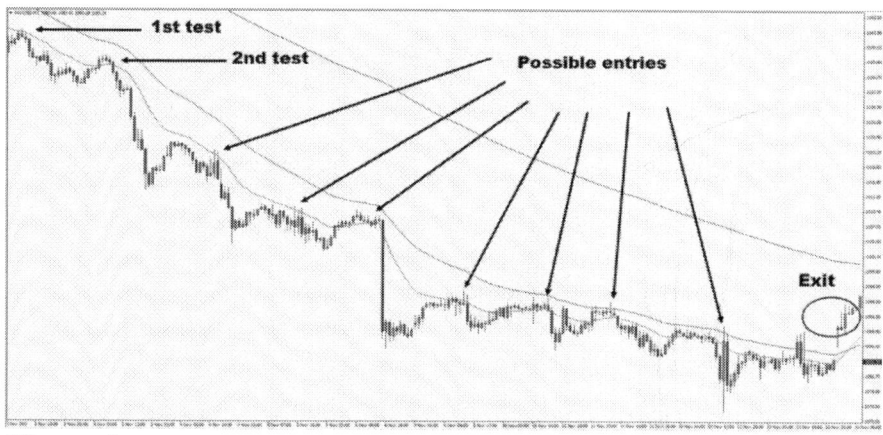

Figure 4
Source:https://my-pull-zone-tradingwithrayne.netdna-ssl.com/wp-content/uploads/2015/11/gold-win.jpg

Chapter 3 – Trend Following: Cross-Over of Moving Averages

Historical Evidence

Now that you know how moving averages work, understanding cross-over will be very easy. In a nutshell, it works in the same way as moving averages, but you will need to follow two lines instead of just one.

Defining Entry Points

Figure 5
Source: Stockcharts.com

This next figure uses two moving averages: short term (over a period of 15 days – red line) and long term (over a period of 50 days – blue line). This is the same as the first chart given above, but with the inclusion of 2 moving averages to determine entry strategy. When the two moving averages converge, it can be used as an entry point. You can also determine when a trend will about to end and reverse by simply plotting down a couple of moving averages on your chart and waiting for a crossover.

Defining Exit Points

What some traders do is that they make their exit once a new crossover has been made or once the price has moved against the position in a predetermined set of pips. Others will exit at a pre-determined stop-loss, because waiting too long may hurt your chances and be too late once a reversal becomes full blown.

Setting up the System

There are several ways to apply cross-over of moving averages, and two common ones are called the Golden Cross and the Silver Cross. In the Golden Cross method, you focus on 200 days of simple moving averages and 50 days simple moving averages. This strategy is widely accepted and more commonly used. On the other hand, the Silver Cross uses 50 exponential moving averages above and 100 exponential moving averages. It was invented on the firm belief that exponential moving averages help to understand market conditions.

While cross-over moving averages work perfectly in a volatile and/or trending market, they don't do too well when the price is ranging. You will get hit with a number of multiple crossover signals and find yourself getting stopped out a lot of times before you get to catch a trend again.

Figure 6

Source: https://tradingstrategyguides.com/exponential-moving-average-strategy/

Chapter 4 – Trend Following: Turtle Trading

Historical Evidence

In 1983, traders Richard Dennis and William Eckhart held the turtle experiment to show that anyone can be taught to trade. They found a group of people and by forking out money from their own pockets, allowed them to trade based on his instructions.

The idea of how turtle trading works lives by the principle of "the trend is your friend". This means buying futures when they are breaking out to the upside of trading ranges and sell short downside breakouts.

Defining Entry Points

Figure 7
Source: https://www.investopedia.com/articles/trading/08/turtle-trading.asp

In this chart, the entry point is established by buying on a new 40-day high. Here are the two ways these "turtles" entered the trade:

- Short-term system based on 20-day breakout

The Turtles entered when the price moved above the high of the last 20 days, or dropped below the low of the last 20 days. Trade was skipped if the prior signal was a winner, such as the price going 2N against the position, before triggering a 10-day profitable exit.

- Longer-term system based on 55-day breakout

The Turtles entered when the price moved above the high of the last 55 days, or dropped below the low of the last 55 days.

The Turtles also did something called pyramiding, which is taking a larger position as the price moves favourably. Once they were in the trade, turtles added one unit to their position each time the price moved ½ N in their favour.

Defining Exit Points

The turtles ended a trade on the breakout, and always did so before the close of the daily market. A breakout is identified when the price of an asset "breaks" trough the high or low of a certain number of days.

At the onset of making the entry, a stop loss is placed 2N below the entry price if long, and 2N above the entry price if short. This served to cut losses if things didn't move favourably after entry. Another exit method is called the Whipsaw, where exit points were being placed at 1/2N away from the entry point. If the price didn't hit the stop-loss point after entry, then the turtles used an N-based system to exit.

- For system 1, the exit was a 10 day low for long positions, and a 10 day high for short positions.
- For system 2, the time period was extended to 20 days for both long and short positions.

It takes a lot of discipline to wait for 10 or 20 day low to exit a position. But avoiding the urge to get out and sticking to the system is what results in huge gains.

Setting up the System

The Turtle Trading System was set up in the early 80's, and there have been a lot of questions raised on its sustainability in the market today. In 1970-1986, this system enjoyed returns of 216%, which was followed by a decline to 10.5% during 1986-2009. However, it did manage to do well from 2004-2016, with max returns of 40%. So while it may not be completely new, it's not entirely obsolete either.

Figure 8
Source: https://vantagepointtrading.com/wp-content/uploads/2017/04/turtle-trading-strategy.jpg

Chapter 5 – Counter-Trend Following: Williams %R

Historical Evidence

The Williams percentage (%R) is a technical indicator which was developed by Larry Williams. It is used to identify whether an asset is overbought or oversold in order to determine possible turning points. It is a single line fluctuating on a reverse scale.

The %R is calculated as follows:

%R = (Highest High – Close) / (Highest High – Lowest Low) X - 100

Nowadays, manual calculations are no longer needed as we have software readily available to us to do the work. The Williams %R is available on most trading platforms such as MetaTrader and ThinkorSwim, as well as on free online charting sites such as Yahoo!Finance and StockCharts.com.

Defining Entry Points

Use a simple 18 day moving average of closing prices. Look for 2 consecutive lows in this 18 day moving average. Then, perform your entry when the price rallies above the highest of the two bars above the 18 day moving average.

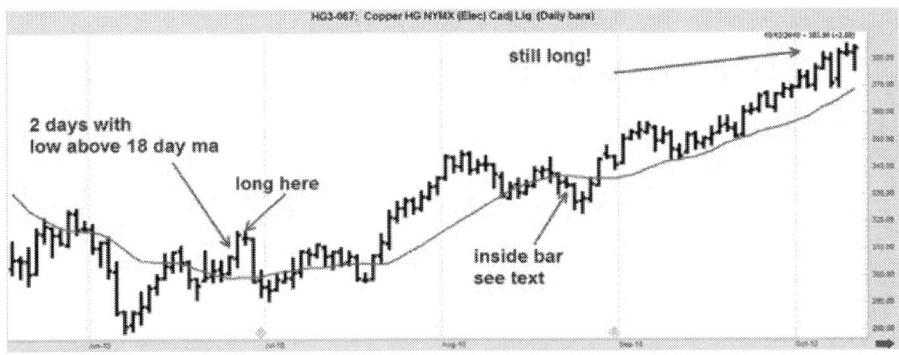

Figure 9
Source: http://williamspercentr.com/lesson6

Defining Exit Points

Place your stop loss for the trade below what your buying price or after an 18-bar sell signal.

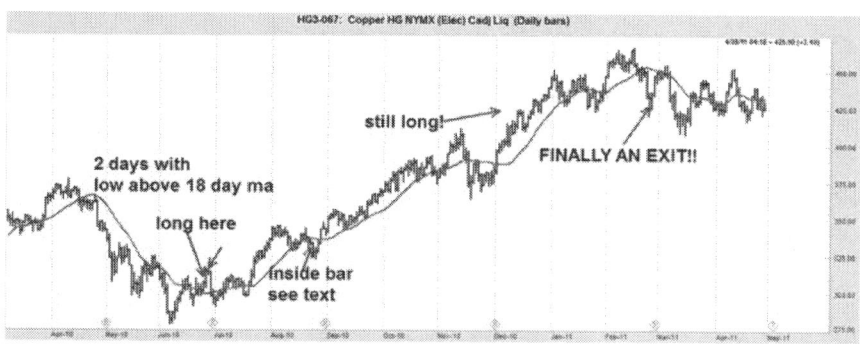

Figure 10
Source: http://williamspercentr.com/lesson6

Setting Up The System

The main goal of the Williams Percentage R is to identify shares that were overbought or oversold, and can be an indicator within trend analysis. Here are some rules:

- If the indicator climbs above -20, the asset may be overbought.
- If the indicator drops below -80, it may be oversold.

Figure 11
Source: https://www.ifcmarkets.com/uploads/docs/Rpercent.jpg

Looking at the extremes in this chart, the indicator may suggest possible turning points:

- Williams Percentage Range signals a possible sell opportunity by crossing the overbought boundary above.
- Williams Percentage Range signals a possible buy opportunity by crossing the overbought boundary below.

While divergence patterns are rare, it may indicate possible weakness:

- Uptrend weakness if the price climbs to a new high but the indicator does not
- Downtrend weakness if the price falls to a new low, but the indicator does not.

In a nutshell, the Williams Percentage R strategy can be summarised as follows:

- Buying when the market is oversold (%R reaches -80 or lower)
- Selling when the market is overbought (%R reaches -20% or higher)

Chapter 6 – Counter-Trend Following: Relative Strength Index

Historical Evidence

The Relative Strength Index (RSI) is undoubtedly one of the most popular indicators in the market. It is basically a measure of how well a stock is performing against itself by comparing the rises and drops during the days. It has a range of 0 to 100; above 70 RSI is considered bullish, meaning the investors are optimistic of the rise in prices, while a reading below 30 is bearish, where the market is in decline and investors are attempting to take profit.

This method may result in several days before trading signals occur, but when they do, there's is a better winning percentage than some of the more active strategies. And since it doesn't need to involve trading every day, it can be used as a supplement to a more active method. This trade works best when trades are signalled in the direction of a long-term trend. When there is no prevailing trend, the signals can be taken in either direction. When the daily ADX is rising, the day trades should be done only in the direction of the trade, and when it is in decline, the trend can go either way.

Defining Entry Points

Entering the trade using the RSI Strategy is very straight forward. You wait for the price to head in the direction of the trade and wait for the first candle to close above the candle that was identified as the previous 50-low candle.

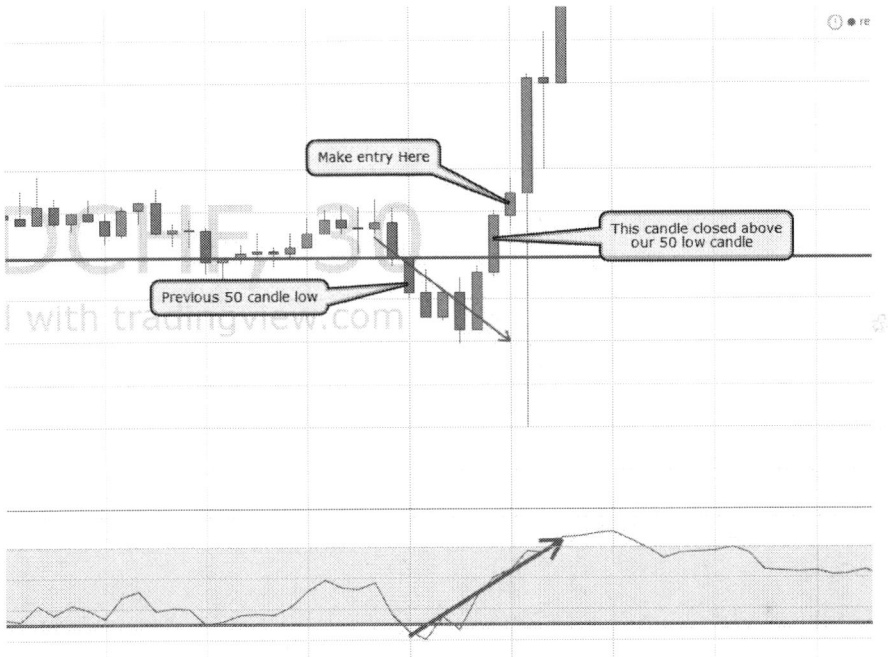

Figure 12
Source: http://tradingstrategyguides.com/wp-content/uploads/2016/12/rC4KBYK-NxBVzUqhlWmnpUTMSVQL-34MjsyG27cDfeLXxeBTUkJd2D8ubH1IsADmfXbJs87s_lRaR3uJk9cm4ZzuOPkoGS84IyWaXThIqV5oo29Mj5yLkX7UWzGTSpWfEay-u01Y.png

Defining Exit Points

As soon as you place your entry, place the stop loss. To place your stop, bump back 1-3 time periods and find a reasonable level to put your stop that makes logical sense.

Figure 13
Source: http://tradingstrategyguides.com/wp-content/uploads/2016/12/FAWNWhsTinlr3pSd8nIxIfWALIRxcEBzvIx7ZhrtKPi2QtuGwlgN3MECJllQwU6zHqx5V-TR4hm2UqWS75PqTw2yCkhTphOWvEiGJB7S_yxojts4QnhZB4-hrGdqzX8Lf1Fxl5DO.png

Follow at least a 1 to 3 profit vs. risk level. This will ensure that you are maximising your potential to get the most out of this strategy.

Setting Up The System

Here are several points in order to set up this system:

- Find the pair that is showing a high in the last 50 candlesticks. Or depending on the trade, identify the low.
- Once we find 50-candle low, we need it to be coupled with RSI reading of 20 or lower. If it's a high, it needs to be coupled with the RSI reading of 80 or higher.
- Wait for a second low price candle to close after the previously identified first one.
- Enter the trade by waiting for a candle to close above or below the first candle you have previously identified.
- Place a stop loss immediately after gaining entry.

Chapter 7 – The Secrets to Day Trading Success

While trading systems vary and can be used in a multitude of ways, having a proven, reliable strategy is one of the single most important factors in the success of day trading. But even when armed with the best strategies, you can still potentially lose a lot of money. And this has nothing to do with incompetence, luck, or the system itself. The art and science of day trading relies on experience, good money management, discipline, and guidance. By examining the pitfalls of trading, you will be able to identify why most traders fail, thus learning from these mistakes and knowing how to avoid them.

- Learn to identify the direction of the market

As an effective day trader, one should learn how to pinpoint when the market is going up or when it is going down. Take advantage of trendlines and educate yourself as much as you can. By properly predicting these trends, you will have a higher chance of being able to make a successful entry, and a profitable exit.

- Don't be greedy

While being in the trading industry makes it difficult not to be greedy, one should exercise a certain kind of self-control and discipline. Day trading isn't a quick-rich strategy – rather, it is built on consistent, small wins. Fortunes are built on the accumulation of the small wins and it takes experience, patience, and determination in order to get there eventually.

- Always know when to exit

Losses may be a part of day trading, but there should be a limit as to when you are giving away too much "room" for these shrinking values. Make it a point to ensure that your average loss should be always be smaller than your average win, because it's the only way to ensure you're still making small profits even if your winning percentage is only 50%.

- *Avoid trading in the wrong markets*

Stay away from a market that is only moving sideways. Instead, trade on those that are moving either up or down. Refrain from focusing on only one kind of market or only on certain stocks.

- *Solidify your trading strategy*

This cannot be stressed enough – having a solid trading strategy is the most important thing you need to work on in order to come to trading prepared, and well-informed. Without it, you are just basically gambling. Remember that trading involves risks, albeit calculated ones at that.

- *Control your emotions*

Being greedy, fearful, panicky, indecisive, or too excited can take a toll on your trading style. In order to effectively implement your strategy, the best way is to just stay calm. Don't allow your emotions to take control over you.

- *Don't Overtrade*

Many day traders think that the more they trade, the more chance they have in hitting the perfect trade that will allow them to gain higher profits. Most traders trade out of greed, and some out of revenge to get back the money they've lost. There are even those that will continue to trade out of sheer boredom just because the market isn't moving the way they want. Whatever their reasons might be, try not to follow suit. Make a trade, stick to it, and exit appropriately. Don't enter everything all at once.

Conclusion

Now that you've reached this part of the book it's time to give yourself a pat on the shoulder. Throughout the course of this book, you've learned valuable information that will help you on your way to becoming a successful day trader. Now that you know what to do, the next and most important step is to put it into practice. You can have the best trading strategy, the right mindset and attitude, but without practice you will be thrown into the pit unguarded. So after you've identified the trading strategy that suits you the most, it's now time to take action. Be confident in the things you have learned, follow your plan, and control your emotions. I wish you nothing but the best in your day trading journey.

-- Leigh Vernon

Investing Psychology for Beginners
BOOK TWO

Leigh Vernon

Text Copyright © [Leigh Vernon]

All rights reserved. No part of this guide may be reproduced in any form without permission in writing from the publisher except in the case of brief quotations embodied in critical articles or reviews.

Legal & Disclaimer

The information contained in this book and its contents is not designed to replace or take the place of any form of medical or professional advice; and is not meant to replace the need for independent medical, financial, legal or other professional advice or services, as may be required. The content and information in this book has been provided for educational and entertainment purposes only.

The content and information contained in this book has been compiled from sources deemed reliable, and it is accurate to the best of the Author's knowledge, information and belief. However, the Author cannot guarantee its accuracy and validity and cannot be held liable for any errors and/or omissions. Further, changes are periodically made to this book as and when needed. Where appropriate and/or necessary, you must consult a professional (including but not limited to your doctor, attorney, financial advisor or such other professional advisor) before using any of the suggested remedies, techniques, or information in this book.

Upon using the contents and information contained in this book, you agree to hold harmless the Author from and against any damages, costs, and expenses, including any legal fees potentially resulting from the application of any of the information provided by this book. This disclaimer applies to any loss, damages or injury caused by the use and application, whether directly or indirectly, of any advice or information presented, whether for breach of contract, tort, negligence, personal injury, criminal intent, or under any other cause of action.

You agree to accept all risks of using the information presented inside this book.

You agree that by continuing to read this book, where appropriate and/or necessary, you shall consult a professional (including but not limited to your doctor, attorney, or financial advisor or such other advisor as needed) before using any of the suggested remedies, techniques, or information in this book.

Table of Contents

BOOK ONE: 5 Expert Systems to Navigate the Stock Market ...1

Introduction 17

Chapter 1 - What You Should Know About Day Trading 18
- The Day Trader..............18
- Your Trading Strategy 20
- Analysing Trading Systems 22
- Selecting Your Market..............22
- Selecting Your Time Frame 24
- Selecting A Trading Style..............24
- Defining Entry Points 25
- Defining Exit Points 25

Chapter 2 – Trend Following: Moving Averages 27
- Historical Evidence..............27
- Defining Entry Points 28
- Defining Exit Points 28
- Setting Up The System 28

Chapter 3 – Trend Following: Cross-Over of Moving Averages 31
- Historical Evidence..............31
- Defining Entry Points 31
- Defining Exit Points 32
- Setting up the System 32

Chapter 4 – Trend Following: Turtle Trading 34

Historical Evidence 34

Defining Entry Points 34

Defining Exit Points 35

Setting up the System 36

Chapter 5 – Counter-Trend Following: Williams %R 37

Historical Evidence 37

Defining Entry Points 37

Defining Exit Points 38

Setting Up The System 38

Chapter 6 – Counter-Trend Following: Relative Strength Index 40

Historical Evidence 40

Defining Entry Points 41

Defining Exit Points 41

Setting Up The System 42

Chapter 7 – The Secrets to Day Trading Success 43

Conclusion 46

What are Cognitive Biases? 57

Chapter 1 - Stubbornness 59

Anchoring Bias 59

    Case Study 59

    Your Learning Curve 60

Confirmation Bias 61

- Case Study 61
- Your Learning Curve 61

Post Purchase Rationalism 62
- Case Study 62
- Your Learning Curve 62

Chapter 2 - Fear 63

Loss Aversion Bias 63
- Case Study 63
- Your Learning Curve 63

Recency Bias 64
- Case Study 64
- Your Learning Curve 64

Inaction Inertia 66
- Case Study 66
- Your Learning Curve 66

Chapter 3 - Greed 67

Hyperbolic Discounting Bias 67
- Case Study 67
- Your Learning Curve 67

Chapter 4 - Confidence 69

Illusion of Control (Outcome Bias) 69
- Case Study 69
- Your Learning Curve 70

Hindsight Bias 70
    Case Study 70
    Your Learning Curve 70

Bias Blind Spot 71
    Case Study 71
    Your Learning Curve 71

Chapter 5 – Affect Heuristics 72

Bandwagon Bias 74
    Case Study 74
    Your Learning Curve 74

Ambiguity Effect 75
    Case Study 75
    Your Learning Curve 75

Attribution Bias (Illusory Correlation) 76
    Case Study 76
    Your Learning Curve 76

Social Proof Bias (closely linked to Bandwagon Bias) 77
    Case Study 77
    Your Learning Curve 79

Contrast Bias (Decoy Effect) 80
    Case Study 80
    Your Learning Curve 80

Monte Carlo Fallacy (Gambler's Fallacy) 81

- Case Study 81
- Your Learning Curve 81

Clustering Bias 82
- Case Study 82
- Your Learning Curve 82

Authority Bias 83
- Case Study 83
- Your Learning Curve 83

Hot Hand Bias 84
- Case Study 84
- Your Learning Curve 84

Martingale Bias 85
- Case Study 85
- Your Learning Curve 85

Deformation Professionelle Bias 86
- Case Study 86
- Your Learning Curve 86

Conclusion 87

Glossary of Terms 88

Introduction 100

Chapter 1 - Learning the Basics 101
- The Forex Market 101
- Getting Started on Forex Trading 103

    Placing an Order 104

  Training for Success 105

    Trading Platforms 106

Chapter 2 - Understanding Technicalities 109

  The Principal Currencies 109

  Forces that Drive the Foreign Exchange Market 111

    Gross Domestic Product 111

    Current Events 111

    Industrial Production Report of the nation 111

    Consumer Price Index 113

    Retail Sales Report 113

  How to Understand and Predict Price Movements 113

    Short-term predictions 114

    Long-term predictions 115

Chapter 3 - Forex Trading Systems 117

  Simple Moving Average 117

  Moving Average Convergence Divergence 121

  RSI – Relative Strength Index 123

Chapter 4 - Secrets to Becoming a Successful Forex Trader .. 128

  Characteristics of Successful Investors and Traders 128

Chapter 5 - Glossary of Terms 131

Conclusion 133

What are Cognitive Biases?

"I think, therefore, I am dangerous."

Man has long held the advantage of being able to use reasoning, which primarily sets us apart from all other creatures on earth. Being able to think ahead and determine the consequences of our actions allow us to make sound decisions in order to avoid situations that can bring us personal harm. However, research attributes 90% of what happens in our brain to our subconscious. This means that a large majority of thinking, decision-making and actions happen without us being aware. The brain may dictate our actions but majority of what goes inside our head is outside of our direct control. Pretty crazy, right?

In fact, many of the decisions that we think are within our direct control really aren't. For example, buying decisions all happen in our subconscious mind. When we make a decision to purchase something, it is the result of an emotional impulse. At a precise moment in time, we desire and therefore must have an item. The conscious mind only comes into play later on. This is the time when we try to justify and rationalize our actions for buying a particular item.

In the same way, traders are often faced with a lot of situations where fast decision-making is imperative. Even if there was an objective approach to begin with, traders usually make erroneous mental shortcuts when it comes to making an investment. They can often be led to make poor decisions based on the order of the information they receive, or perhaps under unique personal circumstances while making a particular decision. Because of these factors, it is important to be mindful of these cognitive biases that arise in order to reach an optimal investment judgment.

Traders rarely have an advantage in terms of technical knowledge or environmental benefit. However, if one has the ability to see the truth before him rationally, and to see facts for how they truly are, then they gain a priceless advantage. If there is a secret to success in trading, it's this: execution is everything. You may have all the technical skills, a proven strategy, and know-how in the world, but the ultimate marker is how you close the decision-making phase. This book will help you become more self-aware of the cognitive biases that plague a trader, and allow you to see the consequences of them. While being biased isn't at all fatal, it can be a huge obstacle to your goal of trading successfully.

Chapter 1 - Stubbornness

Stubbornness has long been a problem with some traders who refuse to change their views, even though the situation changes for the better or worse. Often, we make decisions based on what we think is right i.e. emotionally led rather than relying on the hard facts presented to us during a trade.

What You Can Do

There are several ways to overcome stubbornness as a cognitive bias. It requires one to not hold on to any long-held beliefs, but instead focus on analyzing data and executing based on what the market is telling you. Cutting your losses may be admitting defeat, but limiting the damage is far more important than protecting your ego. This also frees up an opportunity to reinvest somewhere else. It is far easier to recoup your losses in a trade when a stock has momentum, as opposed to waiting for the tide to turn on a sinking ship.

Anchoring Bias

Case Study

Bob starts off his trading day by spotting a bullish trend in the market. He is convinced that the bulls will take full control for the rest of the day. Although the market shows signs of exhaustion later on, Bob is essentially anchored to the information glimpsed from the strong bullish thrust first seen at the start of his day. After many trades, he finally realizes that he has only spent the day fighting the market, all because he was anchored to the positive start.

Your Learning Curve

Does anchoring affect traders? It absolutely does! Everything we do is based on price and value, and we're constantly trying to determine and evaluate the price of our chosen trade and if it's going up or down. Anchors such as the first piece of information we get stuck with get in the way of our objectivity, much like a horse wearing blinkers. When we see a particular stock gaining momentum at the beginning, we think the only way is up.

Listen to what the market is telling you. Strike a balance between looking back in time for support and resistance when executing technical analysis, but also look for additional clues and indicators that may turn the tide. This can be a delicate balancing act, one that requires you to analyze historical data. Just remember, always use past information as a guideline, not an unwavering fact that cannot be altered.

Take control of the anchors themselves. Forget about profit targets, maximum losses, best entry prices, or any other price-based numbers. Even if a trade works exactly the way you want it to go, it doesn't guarantee that any of these targets will be reached. Learn to anchor on execution instead.

Confirmation Bias

Case Study

Bob is trying out a new trading strategy, and decides to increase his variance by participating in ten trades. Among the ten, 8 are losers, and 2 are winners. Subconsciously, Bob downplays the significance of the losers, focusing purely on the 2 profitable trades. Bob convinces himself that the new strategy works and that the losers will eventually recover, even though the bigger picture says otherwise.

Your Learning Curve

Confirmation bias is an example of selective perception, a way of filtering information. But instead of seeking out the negative, it glorifies the positives and makes the success larger than life. Everyone loves being right, so naturally we seek out any information that reiterates that the move that was executed was the right move.

In its logical conclusion, confirmation bias lets traders see trades that just aren't there. The slightest hint of something that looks like a winner already has you jumping in with both feet, diving head-first. But this bias hides the real truth, convincing you that the long trade you just made is really working out, and that the falling price is nothing more than a retracement.

So how do you beat something you are inherently blind to? Flipping charts help – and I mean really physically flipping them. Imagine entering a trade but it doesn't go the way you expect it to. According to your detailed strategy plan, you should pull out and exit, even if it means taking a loss. Flipping a chart helps you see what is really there, instead of what you want to see. By doing this, you are confusing the bias, allowing you no more excuses to stay in the trade. You can quickly exit with a small loss, rather than letting the trade get away from you and turn into a potentially bigger let down.

Post Purchase Rationalism

Case Study

Bob waits patiently and observes the market intently. He refrains from making sub-optimal trades, convincing himself that if he waits long enough, he would find that one perfect trade of the day.

And then it arrives. Bob takes it without hesitation. In his mind, he is convinced that he is the epitome of an ideal trader – patient, calm, observant, and strategically wise. But after getting into a long position, post-purchase rationalization comes in. Bob has placed a considerable amount of time and effort into finding this trade, so much that he forgoes the warning signs from the very start. He refuses to accept that while it did have a potential chance to shine, it is slowly shaping up into a losing trade. As a result, he gave up many chances to exit with smaller gains. In the end, the market plummets, and the small gains became a substantial loss.

Your Learning Curve

After buying something, traders tend to rationalize and prove that the purchase is right. This is especially true for expensive purchases. We do not want to admit that we purchased in bad judgment after spending all that time and effort to research. Do not try to rationalize your trade only after you've made the purchase. That justification should have been done before entering a trade.

Chapter 2 - Fear

Fear is our number one driver for survival. Long before humans have developed the ability to think logically, fear has already kept our ancestors alive, making them seek shelter and protect their loved ones.

Fast forward to a thousand years later – man has developed a bigger brain and incredible feats of logic and reasoning, but fear still plays an integral part of our most primal emotions. In trading alone, fear renders us unable to execute, despite having well thought-out plans.

What You Can Do

This emotion is so deeply ingrained in humans that it's hard to eliminate it completely. The best thing you can do is accept the reality and make it work to your advantage instead. Fear can sometimes override pure logical thinking, but as long as you focus on the facts laid out before you, you can still make a sound decision and be in the driving seat.

Loss Aversion Bias

Case Study

Bob is in a long position. The market slowly begins to creep up. But as soon as it does, Bob immediately moves his stop-loss order after reaching the breaking even point. Bob is so relieved he has come out on top that he has forsaken his true profit potential.

Your Learning Curve

The power of fear helps us protect our assets. Inherently, as human beings we don't like to lose things that belong to us. In Bob's case, he fears that the hard-earned profits he has gained will all go to waste if he risks putting them all in a trade. After all, hanging on to assets is much easier than having to reacquire them. Loss aversion thus banks on the power of fear to help protect our assets. In this case, the traders' mantra often goes like this: *"Don't put all your money in the trade or you might lose it!"* This is why you should always trade only with disposable income, being prepared to potentially lose in order to gain.

Loss aversion can obviously affect your trading performance in more ways than one. It inhibits traders from taking the risks that come with doing business, when in fact business is all about taking risks. Traders eventually come to an epiphany when they realize that not taking risks leads to losing too much profit.

Moving to use your break-even stops is a natural instinct and feels right. It validates the fact that you are a rational trader. But that's not what trading is all about. This course of action is often not the best, given the context of the market you are in.

Recency Bias

Case Study

Bob has been trading by executing pullback trades. However, on this particular day, he experienced 3 consecutive losses, and concludes that pullback trades are a sure-fire way to lose profit. Because of this, he switches to trading range-break outs.

Bob fails to see the bigger picture of making most of his profits from pullback trades because of these recent losses. But by turning to a trading range break-out, he could be giving up a valuable edge in his tested trading style.

Your Learning Curve

Our brains usually prioritises and amplifies the most recent experiences. In Bob's case in the above scenario, he manifests over-learning from the recent losses. This is typical of many traders who avoid trades that remind them of recent losses when trying to improve trading results.

While reviewing trades and learning from them is crucial, traders shouldn't examine and draw conclusions from them too often. Instead of learning from recent experience, learn from your trading results over a more extended period. Make sure that you have a larger sample of trades across a longer period, before you draw hasty conclusions.

Inaction Inertia

Case Study

Bob missed an opportunity to exit from a bearish market. He could have left with a moderate gain but left it too late in hopes of greater profit. As a result of him holding onto his stocks, he eventually loses the uphill battle and forfeits all his profit, and even enters the deep red territory. When he finally gets an opportunity to cut his losses, he gets out and never enters the market again.

Your Learning Curve

Humans have a tendency to think and reflect upon the past, which usually prepares for future decisions. Inaction inertia is a bias that often plagues not only traders, but the general population as a whole. Think about the time when you missed out on a sale or a promotion. The moment the sale was lifted, those discounted items seemed less attractive. This is because of the perceived reduced value of the product, setting our expectations at a lower baseline. Foregoing an attractive opportunity decreases our willingness to go after subsequent opportunities.

Avoiding ruing missed opportunities and the lost counterfactual outcomes. Instead, be more productive and actively seek out potential ways to bounce back by identifying profitable trades to enter.

Chapter 3 - Greed

Greed is everywhere. While it is good to aim high and be ambitious, you should always keep your objectives in check and shape your trading strategy when new data comes into play. Knowing when to take profit and when to let the profit run is the crucial difference between a winning and losing trader. Having a bigger profit can help to offset the inevitable small losses that will occur now and then. Just remember, you can be a profitable trader with 2 winners (big wins) and 8 losers (small losses).

What You Can Do

As traders, one should always be fully aware of the risks involved. A highly volatile stock can reap bigger benefits and is more exciting, but it requires more time as you have to pay close attention to its fluctuations. One also needs a good understanding of exponential growth, as in the case of hyperbolic discounting, in order to properly judge whether the benefits or now outweigh the potential merits in the future.

Hyperbolic Discounting Bias

Case Study

Bob is beaming in front of his monitor, looking at the great paper profits his holdings currently have. He decides to cash in for quick profit so that he can spend it on that home cinema system he has been dying to buy, not realising that if he had more patience his profit would have doubled. Cashing out then would allow him to get both the home cinema system and a powerful TV projector to go with it.

Your Learning Curve

This is what hyperbolic discounting boils down to: making a decision now about the value of something that be altered in the future. Hyperbola is a Greek term for excessive, and in this case, Bob had the tendency to over-value what was being offered now than what would be available later. This desire for instant gratification, of having the need to have the profits in your hand right now, can be very costly indeed. This can make the difference between a winning or losing day. This also ties in to the loss aversion bias mentioned earlier, where the trader cashes in because he is also afraid to lose his profits. Fearful trading is a definite no-go because this inhibits you to make optimum decisions, which is the name of the game.

There is also the false sense of security when it comes to calculating opportunity costs. You might think you made $1000 in a couple of hours and it might take the rest of the day in order to make $1000 more. As a result, you cash out and enter another trade which looks like it is about to explode. The key difference here is momentum in the former and speculation in the latter. You already have history on your side in the first case, and you should ride the wave until you see visible signs of exhaustion. At this point you can exist safely since you have safety nets in place. Giving up momentum for speculation does not seem wise in the grand scheme of things.

Hyperbolic discounting also equates to the flawed ability to judge value over time. You do not want to be the person who has hyperbolic discounting bias, or you will soon find your wealth building project screeching to a halt sooner rather than later.

Chapter 4 - Confidence

If we were to be realistic about all the enormous challenges the world has to offer, it would be more than enough to make us want to give up and submit. A defeatist attitude will get you nowhere, but similarly on the other end of the spectrum it is not good to be overconfident. The latter breeds complacency which can lead to naivety. When looking at trading charts, for example, our brain tends to show us what we want to see, rather than what we should see. A stock which has a constantly rising price gives one a reassuring confidence, but in turn causes us to neglect that the upward gap jumps in price are actually diminishing readily (indicating that momentum is being lost).

What You Can Do

Our built-in optimism has a tendency to let us see what we'd like to see instead of what's really there. A dose of reality through signals and trading history or charts can help ground us. It is great to be confident in making a trade, but not at the expense of hard facts. Remember that trading relies on a good strategy, and looking back to align with your chosen trading style will trump any misguided decisions that might be made.

Illusion of Control (Outcome Bias)

Case Study

Bob thinks that he can control if his next trade is profitable due to his past few successful trades. As a result, he breaks his comfortable limit and invests more than one-third of his bankroll in his trading account. Unfortunately, things don't go his way and his trading portfolio takes a big hit, undoing everything he has done in the last few days. In this instance, Bob fails to realise that by thinking he can control the outcome of the trade, he is indirectly misguided in thinking he can control the market which no one clearly has the ability to do so.

Your Learning Curve

Illusion of control is the cognitive bias that is essentially a combination of confirmation bias and illusory correlation. Also known as outcome bias, it is the tendency to make irrational decisions based on recent outcomes, rather than focus on the quality of the decisions themselves.

This cognitive bias makes us think that we can control events when we actually can't. Recognising that we have no control over the market is the first step in managing our risk. Instead of seeking certainty and control, seek to be comfortable in uncertain situations beyond your control. So what are these things that we can have control over?

You can definitely keep your emotions in check, resulting in logical decisions rather than emotionally clouded ones. Hone your discipline, for the mind is the only thing we can ever dream of controlling.

Hindsight Bias

Case Study

Bob has studied the charts well enough to notice the chart patterns that lead to a bullish market. In his head, he has internalized the facts and seemed very confident in being able to pinpoint the exact trends when it happens. But as soon as it does, he never even noticed.

Your Learning Curve

Humans are almost always susceptible to hindsight bias, the feeling of knowing it all along when you clearly don't. It is human nature to want to feel good and forget about bad experiences. This is because our minds distort the truth so easily, unless we record it immediately before the mid gets the incentive to do so. This is why even the most discretionary traders experience difficulties in real time. They rely on their confidence and ability too much or they are unable to trust their own read of the market.

As a trader, your best shot at overcoming hindsight bias is to focus on ex-ante records. You aim here is to improve trading results, by refining your training edge which is determined by your trading style.

Bias Blind Spot

Case Study

After reading a book on cognitive biases, Bob watches his friend Jane trade. He acutely notices the biases she employs as she makes her selected trades. In his mind, he believes she made the wrong decision for several trades. He goes back to review his own trading decisions and finds fewer biased decisions. But this isn't because he isn't biased at all – but because he was affected by the bias blind spot.

Your Learning Curve

What is the bias blind spot? It is when you spot biases in other people but fail to recognise your own. In order to find your own cognitive biases, ask the opinion of another trader or a friend. We all have blind spots when we look at ourselves – it is much easier to look on from an objective viewpoint.

Chapter 5 – Affect Heuristics

Heuristics are a set of simple, efficient rules in which people use to form judgements and decisions. They are mental shortcuts that we use to conserve effort and energy from the mental workout decision-making entails. Unfortunately, these can pose a drawback, most especially when trading.

It may not come as much of a surprise at all that emotions influence a large part of decision-making, both big and small. You may even notice that you are more likely to take risks or try new things when you are happy, but the less likely when you're feeling down and sad. Heuristics biases are most obvious when you're relying on "gut feeling" to make decisions.

Affect heuristics often lead to quick decisions without the resource-intense process of gathering information or the weighing of pros and cons.

What You Can Do

Affect heuristics can largely influence your trading strategy. Researchers have concluded that when you are in a positive state, you are more likely to perceive an activity as having high benefits and low risks. Conversely, if your emotional state is negative, you are more inclined to see the activity as being low in benefits and high in risks. So what can you do to prevent emotions from contributing to poor decision making?

First of all, self-awareness needs to be in order. Often, simply being aware of the phenomenon helps. If you can realise that you are easily swayed by your emotions, you will be better equipped to make more objective and clear-minded decisions in the future.

Whenever you are faced with a difficult decision during an intense, emotional moment, try talking to yourself in the third person.

Addressing yourself in the third person can help you calm down and see things clearly. This strategy can then help prevent bad decisions made during the heat of a moment.

Bandwagon Bias

Case Study

Bob hears it everywhere. From the news, to that television, to gurus, and all those never-ending forums.

"The bullish market will stop soon!"

He then looks at his charts. Using his technical tools, he doesn't spot any signs of the bullish market ending soon. Nothing bearish at all, and even more bullish clues. Could he have made a mistake?

But because everyone is saying the same thing over and over again, he convinces himself that it must be true, despite the clues he found that proves otherwise. Thus, he sells all his long positions. He has already succumbed to the bandwagon bias, choosing to follow the herd instead of his own analysis.

Your Learning Curve

Humans tend to do things that everyone else is doing, even if there seems to be no logical reason for doing it. This is called herd mentality. The masses may be right, or they may be wrong, but whatever the case, you are probably wrong if you think that something is right only because everyone seems to say so.

In order to avoid the bandwagon, try to stay far enough that you cannot jump on it. If you can rely on your technical tools, do so without listening to commentaries or the news.

Ambiguity Effect

Case Study

Bob is faced with a choice between two trades, one that is new and one that he has never encountered before. He is weighing up the probability of profit, unsure of which trade he should enter. He wants to try something new, risking the probability of a more sure and tested trade. But his natural tendency to avoid choices where not all the facts are known prevents him form doing so. In the end, he chooses not to venture into the new and unknown trade.

Your Learning Curve

The trading business is all about taking risks – the unknown is our bread and butter. We deal in probabilities, not in certainties. Unfortunately, the ambiguity effect bias is deeply ingrained in our natural systems, because it is a form of self-preservation against the unknown.

The first thing to remember when dealing with ambiguity bias is that the outcome of the trade is irrelevant. As traders, our job is to execute the trade to the best of our abilities, whether it makes money or not. It is simply beyond our control. Keep in mind that the more important thing to take away is as you follow your plan and act on it, you have nothing to fear from the unknown.

The next thing is to move your focus from the unknown to the known. Place emphasis and focus on the parts of the trade set-up that fulfil your criteria, rather than looking at a chart or a financial report. Instead of worrying if the underlying trend is good enough, tick off the things you know to be true. If you still cannot ignore the unknowns or imperfections in a trade set-up, then the final trick is to grade these negatives. Assign a grading system with different levels of importance.

Attribution Bias (Illusory Correlation)

Case Study

Bob has made a few expensive, yet profitable trades in the past. He noticed one common denominator during the days he traded – he was wearing the same blue shirt. Because of this correlation, he immediately associated his luck and success to his new talisman.

In order to extend his successful spell, he makes it a point to continuously wear the same shirt every day. However, on one fateful Tuesday morning, he forgets to have the shirt washed and cleaned, leaving him no choice but to wear something new. Because of the absence of his shirt, Bob feels unlucky and finds it difficult to focus as it takes it toil on his mind. He makes a slew of terrible trade choices, which needless to say puts him in a deficit for the day. He heads home, attributing his "bad luck" to the fact that he wasn't wearing the blue shirt.

Your Learning Curve

You may laugh at this example but you will be surprised at how many superstitious traders there are! As traders, we're always on the lookout for something that will give us a competitive edge. Think about the last time you made a really good trade. What was the weather like during that time? Can't remember? The truth of the matter is that the weather had as much influence over your trading performance as the colour of your hair. And yet, we still affix mystical powers to the success or failure of our trades. If all goes well, it's because you were wearing your lucky tie, or that you were able to catch your ride on time. On the other hand, if everything goes down, it's because it was raining or it just wasn't your day.

Illusory correlation gives us the seeds of poor judgement by being subsequently fed and reinforced with the correlation between aspects of our day to our wins. We try to pin the favourable results of our trades to any reason we can find, because essentially we want to replicate the success. It is also so much more satisfying to have a "winning system", than to just admit that sometimes freak trades just happen.

Attributing success to random events isn't inherently bad. The real problem comes the next time when we see a similar set of circumstances. This can cause us to mistakenly identify "golden opportunities" and dive in blind. Attribution bias also allows us to believe that our failures are due to outside forces. We don't like to admit we are wrong, so if a trade doesn't go the way we want it to, we find something else to take the blame.

The solution to this is to make the correlation work for us. This means letting go of the illusions and working with the real reason for our success or failure – our ability to execute. We can't change the market, but we can execute to the best of our ability. Assume responsibility for everything, even for your losses. As an independent trader, do not shift blame as it doesn't help you progress. Find out what's wrong and do what needs to be improved. Take credit for the right things, for following the rules – but not for your profitable trades. Instead of taking credit for single trades, pat yourself on the back for your consistent profits over a long period of time.

Social Proof Bias (closely linked to Bandwagon Bias)

Case Study

Bob is watching a price chart, waiting for his favourite trading signals to surface. The price is rising nicely, and there is a pretty strong uptrend that can be identified. The mood is upbeat, and this coincides with the market sentiment. Bob gets the distinct feeling that it will continue to rise up in the foreseeable future. Suddenly, the price hits the roof and there is an immediate frenzy. Bob has absolutely no idea why this is happening but he gets an immense feeling of being a part of it. Bob does not want to miss out on this positivity spike and decides to buy as many shares as he can at the current price level. His trading plan goes out the window, for no other reason other than him following the crowd (herd mentality).

Your Learning Curve

Social proof is everywhere. You see in the busy grocery stalls attracting a large crowd, or at a diner where a lot of cars are parked outside. A relative of mine said she chooses her next meal based on how busy the eating place is, even if she didn't know what was on the menu.

Humans hate to miss out. A busy diner has a higher probability of serving good food, or at the very least employ an effective way of marketing. Unless you have figured out a trading strategy that makes decisions based on the activity of a large group of people, stay away from forums or chat rooms. If you're reliant on others to make decisions for you, then what kind of trader are you really? Real traders filter out all the noise and make decisions based on their evaluation of a stock, regardless of market sentiment. If it was so easy to make money, we wouldn't be here. In fact, it is probably better to go against market sentiment rather than follow it. If only the top 10% of traders are profitable ones, then it makes sense to go against the crowd, doesn't it? Overwhelming positive market sentiment can lead to shares being overbought, and vice versa.

Of course, we should always evaluate market sentiment against other data rather than following or opposing it. When you want to try something new, do so in a simulated environment first. You can even test situations first by recording what happened after certain market sentiments before diving in.

Beating social proof bias is all about asking "why" constantly. Learn to question your actions before diving headfirst.

Contrast Bias (Decoy Effect)

Case Study

Bob has been in front of his monitor all day long, waiting patiently for a decent set-up to come along. He has been watching charts move sideways, and finally, a half-decent set-up comes in. Because of the preceding disappointment in the market, all of a sudden this opportunity looks like a diamond in the rough. He grabs it immediately, seduced by its limited appeal. Later on, he dawns on the fact that the trade was in fact a fix-up.

Your Learning Curve

Contrast bias is one of the most commonly employed heuristics. It gives traders a way to reach rapid decisions without spending too much time or effort. Bob was faced with a limited number of choices, and while these were less than the ideal trade, it was the best to that moment in time.

The best way to hack this cognitive bias is to build a library of model trades. With a set of perfect text-book examples for each set-up, we can compare every chart we see against the best of the best. If you try to hold up a model of a perfect set-up against it, you will soon overcome this bias when you see the discrepancy. So keep this model trade beside you when trading. Hold it up against your screen and compare. If you trade based on fundamentals rather than technicals, you can adapt your trade library accordingly. Just remember, if there any no decent trade opportunities in a given day, you don't have to make any trades as you are not obliged to.

Monte Carlo Fallacy (Gambler's Fallacy)

Case Study

Bob liquidates a position after it has gone up following a long series of trading sessions. He does so because he erroneously believes that his string of successive gains makes it less likely for the position to decline.

Your Learning Curve

One of the easiest mistakes to make when trading is thinking that past trades influence future ones. In Bob's case, his line of thinking is incorrect because past failed trades do not influence or change the probability that losses will occur in the future. The Monte Carlo Fallacy is the belief that a certain random event is less likely or more likely to occur, given a previous event or series of events.

This phenomenon is based on learned behaviour, and as such, is shaped by those all-powerful cognitive biases. But through education and revision through affirmations, you can learn to leave this way of thinking behind. Know that the market has no memory as far as individual trades go, and the probabilities are almost always the same in endless variations. Once you have this resolved within yourself, you can successfully overcome this cognitive bias.

Clustering Bias

Case Study

After trading for four consecutive days, Bob noticed that the market went up, up, then down, and down. Thinking he has found a pattern, he has failed to recognise that the stock market's movements don't always follow a certain trend and that this is purely coincidental.

Your Learning Curve

Let's face it – day traders are essentially attracted to clustering like bugs to bright lights. Clustering bias is a type of bias wherein one sees a pattern from a random set or sequence of numbers or events. Humans do not like to feel that they do not have control over their own fate. By associating randomness with patterns, we have the opportunity to establish some sort of self-control.

In order to avoid this bias so deeply rooted in us, try to look for information that proves the pattern wrong instead. Hold up the patterns against a model trade, and examine the differences. This way, if you cannot find any deviations, then it is more likely your hypothesis has a shot at being accurate. The only patterns that can be discerned are technical indicators e.g. a hammer in candlestick charts, and even then they are never 100% accurate.

Authority Bias

Case Study

Bob has established a trading strategy that works for him most of the time, allowing him to profit comfortably. A chance meeting at a café one day brings him together with this trading role model John. Although John uses a different approach to trading, he has become very widely known in the field and has become an inspiration to Bob to model on. Bob gets the chance to converse with John, and John tells him his own way of trading has brought about his current level of success. Although Bob is quite happy with his current strategy, he decides to follow John's example as John's success far outweighs his own. He believes switching strategies will shortcut his route to even bigger success and that he can replicate John's methods and hence outcome.

Your Learning Curve

We all feel a deep-seated duty to obey authority throughout our lives, so when an authority figure makes a request from us, we immediately comply. In theory, this is sound: people with more experience and knowledge in the field will have a better head start. It also means you can be free from the stress and pressures of making decisions, as long as you copy what they do, much like a factory process. Authority bias happens when we believe someone, whether they are right or wrong, just because they are in the position of higher status. In the end, we hold our own opinion in lieu of theirs.

To combat this bias, always look at the strength of the argument, and not the person behind it. Gather the opinion of multiple experts, and see it they are consistent with each other. Dig a little bit deeper before following blindly like a lamb to the slaughter.

Hot Hand Bias

Case Study

Bob is an investor. He has a fund manager who does the trading for him. He knows for a fact that his fund manager has a streak of buying and selling a particular stock. He takes this into account, thinking that the fund manager has a "hot hand" and immediately invests based on the fund manager's track record.

Your Learning Curve

Hot hand bias is the cognitive bias that bases the probability of continued success on past success. As with the previous biases that fall under heuristics, one can overcome hot hand bias by having resolve and revisiting information every now and then in order to keep grounded. Pay attention to the big picture – prior to this sequence of trades, is the fund manager a profitable trader on the whole? Looking at a longer period of time takes all the fluctuations into account, and then one can assess the overall profitability.

Martingale Bias

Case Study

Bob is trading in currencies, which tend to trend. As he enters the market at 2 lots, the price begins to dip. He decides to "double down" to increase his holding to 4 lots, lowering his entry price. Even though he may lose 100 pips on the first lot, he only needs a currency pair to rally or to break even.

Your Learning Curve

Martingale theory relies on consistently doubling up a bet when you lose. Lose, then double your bet; lose again, double your bet even more. It is rooted in the premise that those who regularly lose can't lose all the time based on probability and this is where the trouble begins. It is statistically impossible and for you to be wagering double each time unless you have an unlimited cash supply. Chasing your losses can be a dangerous thing, as gamblers who frequent the blackjack tables can attest to.

As a trader, how do you dispel this cognitive bias? A trader needs to have a good management strategy in place, devoid of emotion, superstition and any other obstacle that is counterproductive. A good background in technical analysis can also be helpful, along with familiarity with the trading system you are using. The Martingale theory does provide a certain value in the Forex market as companies may fall into bankruptcy, but countries rarely do. Educate yourself and familiarise your trading strategy, and you just might be able to make it work.

Deformation Professionelle Bias

Case Study

Bob wants to venture into trading and is excited to do so. He has learned all he can and has studied all the possible outcomes. But Bob is a behavioural psychologist. He thinks he has the advantage of being able to control his reactions due to a larger self-awareness of his actions than the norm. He knows that his emotions play a huge part in decision-making and thus employs all learned strategies he knows from his practice. Unfortunately, by being too aware and careful of his emotions, he fails to take into account the randomness of the market as well as the technical analyses it entails when making a trade. He believes trading is all about action and reaction and that is his only gameplay.

Your Learning Curve

Deformation professionelle is the tendency to look at things from the point of view of your profession, rather than the bigger picture. Its implication is that one's professional training as well as its related socialization often distorts the way one views the world or the situation at hand. Different industries require different skillsets: an expert in all things tech can be a novice when it comes to relationships.

Combating this bias is where the third person perspective truly shines. If you find it difficult to look at things objectively, present the same set of information to a close friend or member of the family and see what they think. This fresh perspective can prove to be refreshing and ultimately gives you more options to explore. Removing the involuntary blinkers can open your eyes to a whole new way of thinking.

Conclusion

Much of what happens inside our brains, as well intentioned as they may be, are working against us when we trade. These ingrained biases have been developed and programmed over time. And while there are ways to hack the system and learn to undo them, it can all seem very overwhelming at first. I don't expect you to change everything in one go, but tackling one obstacle at a time can do wonders. Every little success is still success, and you have already made the first step by striving to identify these trading biases.

Ultimately, improvement is a constant process. Committing yourself to a better disposition, coupled with a great strategy and solid trading plan, can enable you to be one step closer to your desired success as a seasoned trader.

-- Leigh Vernon

Glossary of Terms

Bearish Market – Refers to a weak market, one wherein traders think the prices of stock are going to move down.

Break-even – The point at which gains equal the losses

Bullish Market – The opposite of a Bearish Market, referring to a strong market.

Currency Pair – The simultaneous buying and selling of two different currencies in the foreign exchange market (Forex)

Day Trading – This is when a trader places an opening and closing trade on the same stock, on the same day

Entry – The price at which an investor buys an investment

Equity – The ownership of assets after liabilities and debts have been settled

Exit – Point at which the investor sells his shares to realise his gains or losses

Long Position – Occurs when traders are buying shares in the expectation that the asset will increase in value.

Pip – Short for point in percentage, a small measure of change for calculating profits and losses in the **Foreign Exchange market**

Pullback Trades – The falling back of a security's price from its peak

Rally – A period of sustained increases in the prices of stocks, bonds, or indexes

Stock – A type of asset that gives you an ownership stake in a company, allowing you to benefit from a company's assets and earnings

Stop Order – A value representing a limit that traders use to determine when to get out of a trade, mainly used to protect long positions

A Beginner's Guide to Forex

BOOK THREE

Leigh Vernon

Text Copyright © [Leigh Vernon]

All rights reserved. No part of this guide may be reproduced in any form without permission in writing from the publisher except in the case of brief quotations embodied in critical articles or reviews.

Legal & Disclaimer

The information contained in this book and its contents is not designed to replace or take the place of any form of medical or professional advice; and is not meant to replace the need for independent medical, financial, legal, or other professional advice or services, as may be required. The content and information in this book have been provided for educational and entertainment purposes only.

The content and information contained in this book have been compiled from sources deemed reliable, and it is accurate to the best of the Author's knowledge, information, and belief. However, the Author cannot guarantee its accuracy and validity and cannot be held liable for any errors and/or omissions. Further, changes are periodically made to this book as and when needed. Where appropriate and/or necessary, you must consult a professional (including but not limited to your doctor, attorney, financial advisor or such other professional advisor) before using any of the suggested remedies, techniques, or information in this book.

Upon using the contents and information contained in this book, you agree to hold harmless the Author from and against any damages, costs, and expenses, including any legal fees potentially resulting from the application of any of the information provided by this book. This disclaimer applies to any loss, damages, or injury caused by the use and application, whether directly or indirectly, of any advice or information presented, whether for breach of contract, tort, negligence, personal injury, criminal intent, or under any other cause of action.

You agree to accept all risks of using the information presented in this book.

You agree that, by continuing to read this book, where appropriate and/or necessary, you shall consult a professional (including but not limited to your doctor, attorney, or financial advisor or such other advisor as needed) before using any of the suggested remedies, techniques, or information in this book.

Table of Contents

BOOK ONE: 5 Expert Systems to Navigate the Stock Market ...1

Introduction 17

Chapter 1 - What You Should Know About Day Trading 18

    The Day Trader 18

    Your Trading Strategy 20

    Analysing Trading Systems 22

    Selecting Your Market 22

    Selecting Your Time Frame 24

    Selecting A Trading Style 24

    Defining Entry Points 25

    Defining Exit Points 25

Chapter 2 – Trend Following: Moving Averages 27

    Historical Evidence 27

    Defining Entry Points 28

    Defining Exit Points 28

    Setting Up The System 28

Chapter 3 – Trend Following: Cross-Over of Moving Averages 31

    Historical Evidence 31

    Defining Entry Points 31

    Defining Exit Points 32

    Setting up the System 32

Chapter 4 – Trend Following: Turtle Trading 34

Historical Evidence 34

Defining Entry Points 34

Defining Exit Points 35

Setting up the System 36

Chapter 5 – Counter-Trend Following: Williams %R 37

Historical Evidence 37

Defining Entry Points 37

Defining Exit Points 38

Setting Up The System 38

Chapter 6 – Counter-Trend Following: Relative Strength Index 40

Historical Evidence 40

Defining Entry Points 41

Defining Exit Points 41

Setting Up The System 42

Chapter 7 – The Secrets to Day Trading Success 43

Conclusion 46

What are Cognitive Biases? 57

Chapter 1 - Stubbornness 59

Anchoring Bias 59

    Case Study 59

    Your Learning Curve 60

Confirmation Bias 61

    Case Study 61

    Your Learning Curve 61

  Post Purchase Rationalism 62

    Case Study 62

    Your Learning Curve 62

Chapter 2 - Fear 63

  Loss Aversion Bias 63

    Case Study 63

    Your Learning Curve 63

  Recency Bias 64

    Case Study 64

    Your Learning Curve 64

  Inaction Inertia 66

    Case Study 66

    Your Learning Curve 66

Chapter 3 - Greed 67

  Hyperbolic Discounting Bias 67

    Case Study 67

    Your Learning Curve 67

Chapter 4 - Confidence 69

  Illusion of Control (Outcome Bias) 69

    Case Study 69

    Your Learning Curve 70

Hindsight Bias 70
    Case Study 70
    Your Learning Curve 70

Bias Blind Spot 71
    Case Study 71
    Your Learning Curve 71

Chapter 5 – Affect Heuristics 72

Bandwagon Bias 74
    Case Study 74
    Your Learning Curve 74

Ambiguity Effect 75
    Case Study 75
    Your Learning Curve 75

Attribution Bias (Illusory Correlation) 76
    Case Study 76
    Your Learning Curve 76

Social Proof Bias (closely linked to Bandwagon Bias) 77
    Case Study 77
    Your Learning Curve 79

Contrast Bias (Decoy Effect) 80
    Case Study 80
    Your Learning Curve 80

Monte Carlo Fallacy (Gambler's Fallacy) 81

- Case Study 81
- Your Learning Curve 81
- Clustering Bias 82
  - Case Study 82
  - Your Learning Curve 82
- Authority Bias 83
  - Case Study 83
  - Your Learning Curve 83
- Hot Hand Bias 84
  - Case Study 84
  - Your Learning Curve 84
- Martingale Bias 85
  - Case Study 85
  - Your Learning Curve 85
- Deformation Professionelle Bias 86
  - Case Study 86
  - Your Learning Curve 86

Conclusion 87

Glossary of Terms 88

Introduction 100

Chapter 1 - Learning the Basics 101

- The Forex Market 101
- Getting Started on Forex Trading 103

Placing an Order 104

Training for Success 105

Trading Platforms 106

Chapter 2 - Understanding Technicalities 109

The Principal Currencies 109

Forces that Drive the Foreign Exchange Market 111

Gross Domestic Product 111

Current Events 111

Industrial Production Report of the nation 111

Consumer Price Index 113

Retail Sales Report 113

How to Understand and Predict Price Movements 113

Short-term predictions 114

Long-term predictions 115

Chapter 3 - Forex Trading Systems 117

Simple Moving Average 117

Moving Average Convergence Divergence 121

RSI – Relative Strength Index 123

Chapter 4 - Secrets to Becoming a Successful Forex Trader .. 128

Characteristics of Successful Investors and Traders 128

Chapter 5 - Glossary of Terms 131

Conclusion 133

Introduction

The life of a trader can be very challenging, albeit rewarding. Brand new traders all make the same mistakes over and over, not because they don't have what it takes, but because they simply don't know any better. As beginners, everyone else is studying the same thing and thus gives the same results. But it also means they fail like everyone else, making the same mistakes. If you're someone who's thinking about going into Forex trading, then this book is for you. Rather than teach you what to do, your edge will be learning the things not to do before you can consistently be profitable in the live markets.

Forex trading must be approached in the same way as one would approach any other job. A successful trader is one who can acknowledge that losses are a fact of life and every trader at one point or another will experience them. But the market is always going to be there waiting to give you a chance to make money. Every day, about $4 trillion worth of currency is traded daily, making the Forex market the largest financial market operating in the world. Because of this, most people who are new and are just starting out in this business have unrealistic expectations on what they will be able to pull out of the market money-wise on a daily basis. This book will aim to help you adjust your sails and maintain your focus by taking things really slow and absorbing every detail possible before you decide to trade live. Learning this trade will take some time, but with patience, discipline, and an insatiable drive for success, you will find yourself trading successfully very soon.

Chapter 1 - Learning the Basics

The Forex Market

The Forex market can offer great opportunities to people from all walks of life, providing great returns on their investments. Some can even make trading a full-time job or good second incomes. But as with any type of trading, there are also associated risks involved. If one is unable or has failed to understand these risks and make the necessary preparations involved, it is likely to lead to financial losses. In order to maximise returns and minimise losses, one must be equipped with enough "market knowledge" – one that this book is trying to encapsulate.

The Global Foreign Exchange Market, which is also known as forex or FX, represents the platform by which currency from one country can be exchanged into currency from another. Depending on the economic stability or instability of each country, the value of currencies across the globe fluctuates constantly. These fluctuations present opportunities for the traders to make money. Simply put, if a country's economy performs well, it is likely to result in an increase in the value of that currency. On the other hand, if the economy of that country is doing poorly, its currency value decreases. While many things can influence these fluctuations, the main goal of traders is to recognise them and trade accordingly.

In trading stocks and shares, there is a centralised exchange in which securities can be bought and sold. However, the forex market is different. It operates on a distinctly decentralised structure, allowing many institutions and organisations to offer currency transactions at a variety of prices. This provides considerable opportunities for retail traders, actually ensuring that the best possible pricing deals are available at all times.

In the Forex market, there is a certain degree of participants, and they are as follows:

1. Inter-Bank Market

   This includes the world's largest banks and some smaller regional institutions that directly trade between each other using the Electronic Broking Services (EBS) or the Reuters Dealing 300 spot matching.

2. Hedge Funds, Retail Market Makers, and Business Institutions

   Transactions are generally directed through commercial banking partners. These participants utilise foreign exchange mechanisms, either as part of global business operations or for speculative investment purposes.

3. Retail Traders

   This group ranges from day traders who trade every day, to irregular ones who only trade now and then. Costs of trading are much higher as compared to the other 2 tiers, but with the introduction of internet-based retail brokerage, it is much easier to actively participate within the marketplace.

Getting Started on Forex Trading

Many of the techniques used in trading stocks and share are equally applicable to foreign exchange markets. Forex trading also has the particular advantage of the possibility for larger returns on investments as compared to other financial securities. Some of the characteristics in trading in the Forex market include:

- 24-hour Market – You can trade at any time, everywhere, owing to the global nature of the Forex market.

- Commission-free trading

- Liquidity – Due to its sheer size, the Forex market is extremely liquid, meaning there will always be buyers and sellers out there.

- Stops – Most brokers provide guaranteed stops when trading.

- Leverage – Traders can apply leverage to their trades so that they can maximise potential returns.

- Identifiable trends

- Easy access to Market News

Despite the Forex market being open 24 hours a day, there are specific times when it can be of more advantage to trade than at other times. These optimum times occur when there are high transaction volumes and intensive market activity. It is usually during midweek, at a time when there are overlapping markets that are open. Some of the least favourable days to trade are during Mondays (when the market reacts to weekend news and other activities), Friday (low volumes), Weekends, holidays, and when significant news events are happening.

Placing an Order

The exact procedure in which one must place an order will vary slightly from different traders, brokers, and across different trading platforms. But whatever way you do it, you will need to consider some common factors that will form the basis of your trading strategy. These are as follows:

- Which currency pair you wish to trade

- Whether you are going long or going short during a trade

- Check your analysis and make sure that you are confident of where the price could be going

- Check indicators and tools to reinforce your strategy

- Predetermine exit points using support and resistance

- Predetermine a profit target

- Select an order type

- Select the lot size

- Manage the risk associated with trade

This is just an example list of what one might use before making any transactions. Once your order has been executed, it is then essential to monitor the trade and implement the right tools that can help you analyse and keep track of your performance. Forex trading isn't about acting on impulse, but rather on keeping a cool head throughout.

Once the above factors have been identified and considered, it is then vital to stick to your chosen strategy. There will always be times when you hit your profit target and feel that you need to stay in order to make more money potentially. But this method of chasing profits can be dangerous, and by staying in a trade longer than what was originally planned can increase the possibility of being hit by price reversals. Set a stop loss, and stick to it. While losses are part and parcel of trading, you can keep them to an absolute minimum.

Training for Success

Most trading education that is being taught in books and classes are helpful to a beginner, some even more than the others. But it is important to note that learning the right information and not just any information is one of the most critical steps to become a successful market participant over the long term. It is said that the average time frame it takes someone to go from starting with zero knowledge and learning the Forex business to becoming consistently profitable is in a period of 3-5 years. This is the reality. One must learn all the technical aspects, as well as get the first-hand experience, losses, wins, and all, in order to fully understand how you should approach trading in the Forex market.

Learn to become familiar with reading charts, price actions, market dynamics, supply and demand trading, and how the trading platform you are using works in your favour, how to execute a position, placing a stop loss and how to set up an exit order on the chosen platform. Adequate preparation is needed, and learning as much as you can is definitely the only way to go. In order to help you get started, know what kind of trader you desire to be. With this information, you can plan out what type of education and training will work for you, especially when you're about to enter the learning phase of the knowledge curve. Although there may be a lot to know, trim it down to only the ones that perfectly match your expectations and the kind of trader you want to be. With this, you can be successful in your chosen strategy.

Trading Platforms

Trading Platforms, more specifically, currency trading platforms help currency traders with Forex trading analysis and trade execution. They are often used in conjunction with equity trading platforms for avid market day traders. In a retail equity trading market, some of the most popular trading software resources include Metastock, Chart Nexus, Amex, NYSE among others. Here, we take a look at some of the pros and cons of the given trading platforms below:

	PROS	**CONS**
Chart Nexus	<ul><li>Great for newbie traders</li><li>Free to use</li><li>Downloads data directly from the Stock Exchange server</li><li>Indicators include: MACD, Moving average, and Parabolic SAR among others</li></ul>	<ul><li>Unable to optimise and edit the formula for indicators; not carried over to the next</li><li>End-of-day data available instead of real-time data</li><li>Adding to portfolio requires you to scroll through alphabetised lists</li></ul>

Nasdaq	<ul><li>Good selection of currency pairs, including crypto coins</li><li>Offer leverage as high as 200:1 to accommodate any trading style</li><li>Free to use</li></ul>	<ul><li>Broker is unregulated</li><li>Uncompetitive spreads</li><li>NeTeller and Skrill are not accepted payment methods, withdrawals subjected to fees</li><li>No information about minimum deposit requirement</li></ul>
NYSE: FXCM	<ul><li>One of the oldest and most recognised names in online currency trade</li><li>Regulated by US SEC</li><li>Active traders can take part in lower spreads</li><li>Available in desktop, mobile, and web versions</li></ul>	<ul><li>Paid platform</li><li>High commission of brokers</li><li>Catalogue of underlying assets is smaller than others</li></ul>
Forex.com	<ul><li>Great mobile experience</li><li>Easy-to-consume data and research</li></ul> Excellent trade execution	<ul><li>Paid platform</li><li>No automated trading</li><li>Cannot trade basic equity or fixed income</li></ul>
MetaStock	<ul><li>Comprehensive for newbies and most</li></ul>	<ul><li>Paid platform</li></ul>

	popular among traders • Powerful analysis tools • Simple and easy platform	• Limited execution of trades from charts and integrated profit and loss analysis

Chapter 2 - Understanding Technicalities

The Principal Currencies

So, does one make money in Forex trading? The objective is to exchange one currency for the other, in the hope that the price of the currency bought will increase in value, compared to the value of the currency sold. The way to achieve this is through the use of a currency pair. Forex trading will always be based upon these two currencies. When making a foreign exchange transaction, you are essentially buying one currency and selling another. The first currency is known as the base currency, while the second is known as the quote currency. The quote currency tells you how many units of that currency are required to buy one unit of the base currency. It also shows you how many units of the quote currency you can receive for every one unit of the base currency sold. For example, if you were to place a buy order for the USD/GBP (US dollar/British pound), you would be buying USD while selling GBP. And in order for you to make a profitable trade, you will need to buy the currency pair in which the base currency has the potential to increase or rise in value, in relation to the quote currency over the period that you hold it for. Alternatively, you would sell the currency pair if you expect the base currency to depreciate relative to the quote currency over time.

Some of the major currency pairs are as follows:

EUR: USD (Euro – US Dollar)

GBP: USD (Pound Sterling – US Dollar)

USD: CHF (US Dollar – Swiss Franc)

USA: CAD (US Dollar – Canadian Dollar)

USD: JPY (US Dollar – Japanese Yen)

EUR: GBP (Euro – Pound Sterling)

EUR: CHF (Euro – Swiss Franc)

AUD: USD (Australian Dollar – US Dollar)

NZD: USD (New Zealand Dollar: US Dollar)

Forces that Drive the Foreign Exchange Market

Investing in the success of a nation's currency means that you are essentially investing in the success of nations themselves. Here are some of the major forces that drive the Foreign Exchange Market:

Gross Domestic Product

The GDP of a nation affects the strength of a nation's currency by weakening or strengthening the net production of the country. It represents the power of the workers' force of a nation, regardless of the percentage of import and export. This is an indicator of the nation's working ethic of its people and their strength of working power.

Current Events

A currency's value is closely linked to the state of affairs of a nation. News can move the market in very extreme ways. For example, political instability can be viewed by traders as greater volatility in the value of a country's currency. In the case of natural disasters, the loss of infrastructures and the decrease in consumer spending can be turned into an economic weakness. The same is true for wars. There's not much that can be done with unexpected events, but I hope that the effects won't be too hard on you and that you can manage the risk.

Industrial Production Report of the nation

While GDP measures the amount of production, the industrial production report measures the efficiency of what is being produced. If the country is efficient, it will have a better rating on this factor than a country that is less efficient. This is because it is generally favourable for a country to have increasing values of capacity and production at such high levels.

Consumer Price Index

The main idea behind the consumer price index is to determine whether a country is making or losing money with what they are producing. Consumer Price Index measures the weighted average of prices of a basket of consumer good and services. This includes food, transportation, and medical care to name a few. Any changes that occur in the CPI are then used to assess price changes that are associated with the cost of living, and it is a statistic that is used frequently in identifying periods of inflation or deflation. It also provides the government with an idea about price changes in the economy.

Retail Sales Report

Retail sales is an aggregated measure of the sales of retail goods over a period of time. This determines what people are spending their money on and how much. It is an important indicator because it estimates the total merchandise sold by taking in sample data from retailers across the country. Consumers represent more than two-thirds of the economy, so traders use this information to gauge the direction of a nation's economy.

How to Understand and Predict Price Movements

As a forex trader, your main goal is to correctly predict future price movements of currency pairs. But this is far from easy, and this is due to the number of factors that influence its movement. While there is a lot to learn about predicting the movements, we can generally classify it into two methods: short-term predictions and long-term predictions.

Short-term predictions

This type of prediction uses tools, such as technical analysis, order flow data, sentiment surveys, and analysing prices of the futures market.

Technical Analysis

In technical analysis, it is generally assumed that historical prices and patterns tend to repeat themselves; thus prices move in trends. This method attempts to identify these trends in its early stages and to trade in the direction of the trend until it reverses. There are many tools used to determine this too, such as chart patterns, trendlines, or support/resistance zones that serve the purpose of recognising trends.

Order Flow Data

This is based largely on the basis of demand and supply, as banks and other large Forex players use the information of their customers' order flow to predict changes in prices.

Sentiment Surveys

These surveys make an effort to sense the wider sentiment of a market participant to predict price movements. If the sentiment becomes increasingly bullish or bearish towards a particular currency, it could rise or fall in the foreseeable short-term.

Futures Market

This is a means of identifying the trends in the price changes, which traders can then use to anticipate how the futures market feel about a certain currency – whether it is bullish or bearish.

Long-term predictions

Exchange rates of currencies tend to go back to their fundamental level of equilibrium in the long term. However, one should keep in mind that no general agreement is used globally on what represents a currency's long-term equilibrium exchange rate. Or how it should be calculated. To explain this, long-term predictions use the Purchasing Power Parity approach (PPP) in order to predict exchange rates in the long run. Other valuation models include the balance of payments approach, monetary approach, interest rate approach, and portfolio approach – all of which take into consideration different approaches in their calculations.

Purchasing Power Parity

This is the approach with the largest following, and it is based on the presumption that the prices of goods and services tend to be equalised among different countries in the long run.

To illustrate, let's say a certain car type and model costs $50,000 in the U.S., and 45,000 Euros in Germany. The EUR/USD exchange rate needed to achieve a PPP equilibrium will have to be $1.11, because of $50,000/45,000 Euros.

If the current exchange rate of EUR/USD is $1.50, then a car buyer from Germany could order a car from the US at $50,000 and pay only 33,333 Euros in his terms, allowing him to save almost 12,000 Euros. With this opportunity, many German car buyers will then choose to buy the car in the U.S., and this increase in demand will eventually return the $1.50 exchange rate towards the equilibrium rate of $1.11.

This approach may be useful, but it does have drawbacks. It mostly works only for tradeable goods, as exchange have an inherent tendency to deviate from their supposed equilibrium level.

Chapter 3 - Forex Trading Systems

In forex trading, the trader generally has two options: manual or automated. What the trader does is look for trading signals either by following and monitoring a computer screen closely (manual) or developing his own tested algorithm for this, which then executes on their own (automatic). No matter the method chosen, it is only up to your individual taste on what works better for you.

In order to trade effectively, one must consider the following things first:

1. Market Selection – where you choose the currency pairs to trade

2. Sizing the position – in order to control the amount of risk taken in each trade, one must determine how large a position is

3. Entry – set of rules on when to enter a trade

4. Exit – set of rules on when to exit a trade

5. Tactics for trading – rules on how to buy and sell the chosen currency pairs, as well as the right techniques for execution that go with it.

Simple Moving Average

As the name suggests, the simple moving average is the most basic concept to learn in the analysis of Forex. Getting the moving average simply means that one adds up all the given values on a specified time period, and divide the total sum by that number of days or hours in which the values were taken. Simply put, it is the mean of values being presented at a certain time.

The purpose of getting the simple average is to help identify trends better. Since it utilises information taken in the past over a long period of time, the graph that one would make becomes smoother over time. It also provides traders with a trend to look out for, so that entry signals can be identified as soon as they occur.

There are two types of averages - long term and short term. They are simply what they're called – an average that is taken over a longer period of time and one that is taken shorter. When these two averages are placed on a chart and graphed, a convergence will eventually occur. If the long-term line starts to go uphill and above the short-term line, it can be an entry signal. On the other hand, if it occurs the other way around, it can mean a downtrend in the market.

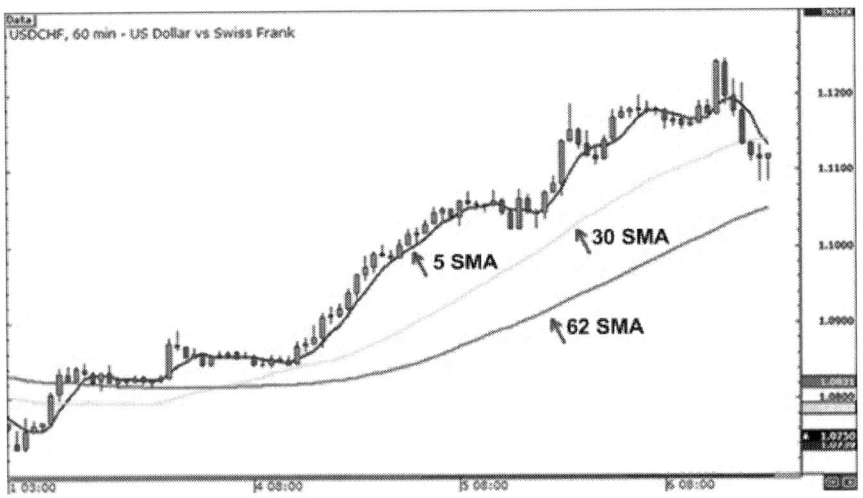

On the graph above, the USD/CHF currency pair is shown to be going on an uptrend. With the current price in place, one will notice that the 62 SMA doesn't really get affected over time. It doesn't have too many changes or spikes.

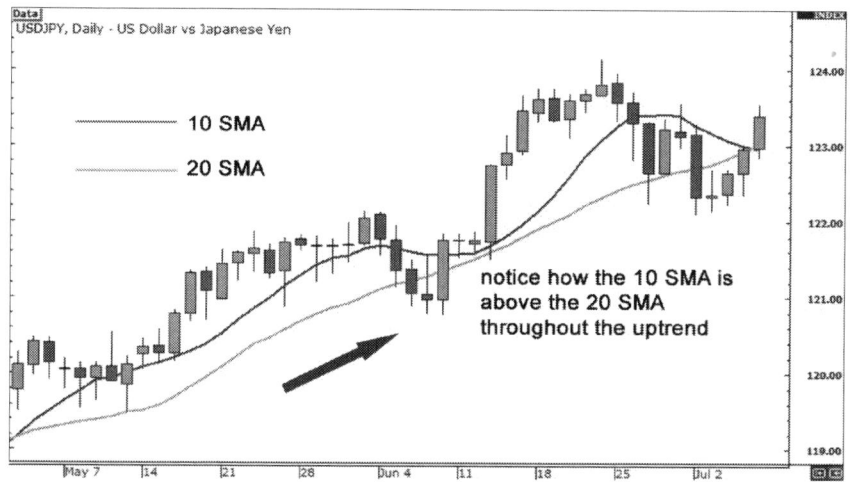

This chart shows us an uptrend, wherein the "faster" moving average should be above the "slower" moving average. In a downtrend, it is vice versa. With this, you can use moving averages to determine whether a pair is trending up or down. It can then help you decide whether to go long or short with the chosen currency.

Entry: Wait for a crossover between moving averages, usually between a long-term average and a short-term average. Once they start to converge or cross over each other, it can be your go signal for entry. Keep in mind that if the moving averages are plotted over a longer period of time, the better your chances of finding a trend.

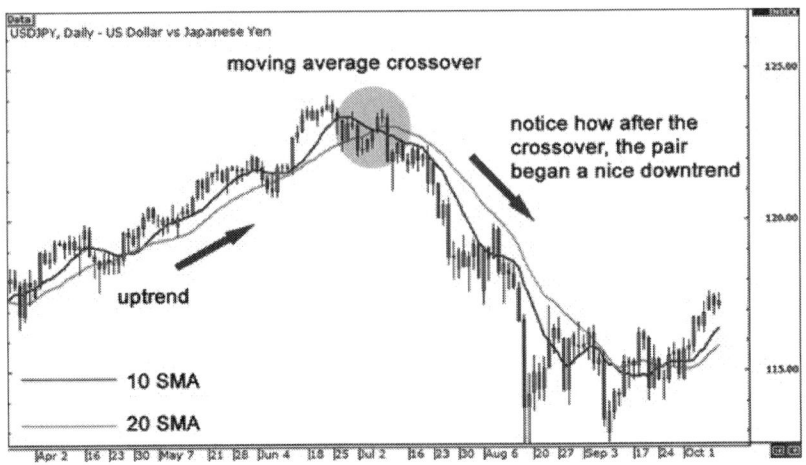

This chart shows a nice uptrend until it topped out at around 124.00 before slowly heading down. In the middle of July, we see that the 10 SMA crossed over with the 20 SMA. This gives you an opportunity to enter.

Exit: Exiting in this strategy requires the trader to pull out as soon as a new crossover happens, or even before that. But because the next crossover may be unpredictable, even with a load of historical data and evidence to back it up, placing a stop loss order is the best way to get around it. It saves you from potential loss and secures the profits already made during the trade.

Moving Average Convergence Divergence

The moving average convergence/divergence (MACD) is an indicator in the Forex market designed to gauge momentum. Apart from identifying a trend, it also measures the strength of a trend and is considered one of the best indicators for Forex.

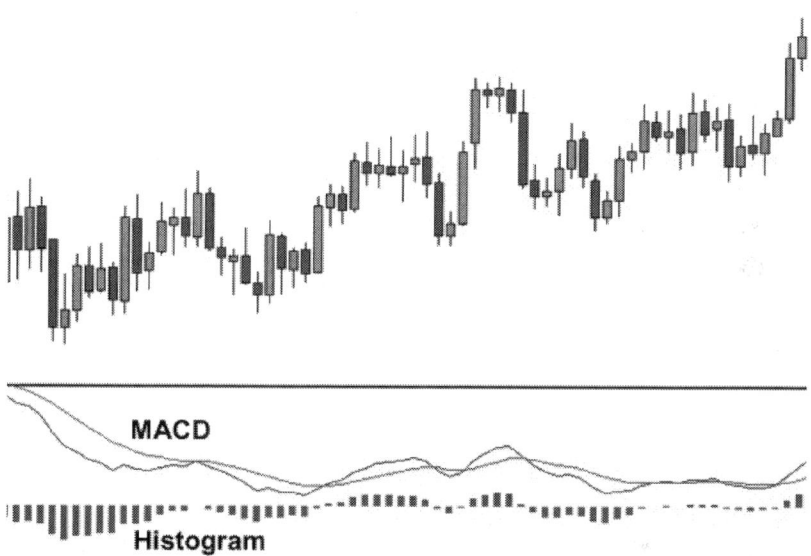

Three numbers are generally seen and used in a standard MACD chart.

These are:

- Faster moving average – the first number of periods
- Slower moving average – the second number of periods
- Moving average of the difference between the faster and slower moving averages – the number of bars used to calculate

To interpret the numbers, it would be something like this:

Faster moving average (10) and slower moving average (26) and the difference between the two averages (9) as seen in the histogram. When the two moving averages move away from each other, the histogram becomes bigger, called a divergence. Conversely, when these two move closer until they meet, this is called a convergence.

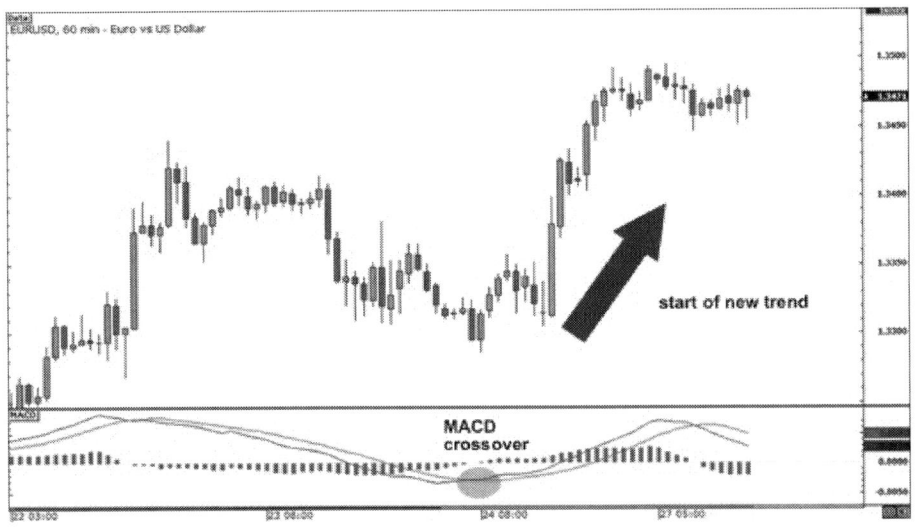

To determine the trend in a MACD, take a look at the chart above. The fast line crossed above the slow line while the histogram disappeared. This suggests that the downtrend will reverse.

Entry: Entry comes when MACD makes a higher low and the next bar ticks up, signalling bullish momentum is growing. Look for the bullish crossovers that occur within 2 days from each other.

Exit: When a bearish divergence occurs, it may be time to exit. Preferably, you want the histogram value to already be or to move higher than zero within two days of placing your chosen trade. But placing stop loss orders are a surefire way to reduce potential losses.

RSI – Relative Strength Index

RSI identifies overbought and oversold conditions in the market. It is called from 0-100, with readings below 30 to indicate oversold market conditions, and readings over 70 to indicate overbought conditions. This is illustrated in the graph below:

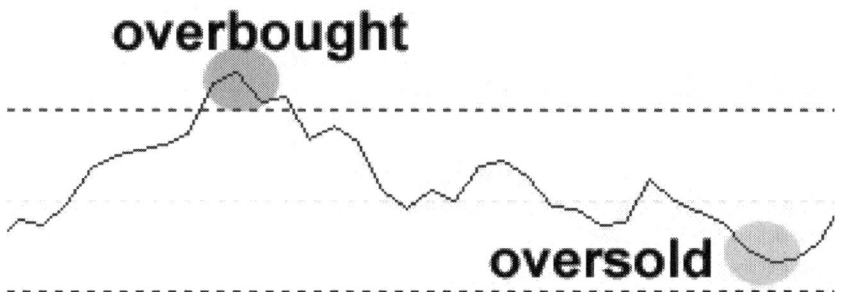

RSI is a very popular tool because it can also be used to confirm formations of coming trends. If you think that a trend is forming, look at the RSI and check whether it is below or above 50. An uptrend means that the RSI is above 50, and a possible downtrend means the RSI is below 50.

At the beginning of the chart above, we can see a possible downtrend forming. Waiting for the RSI to cross below 50 confirms that trend and avoid fake-outs.

Take a look at the chart above that shows the currency pair AUD/USD. First and foremost, the use of the RSI is to find out the buying signal, which is when the price crosses the 30 level. By doing this, traders are basically buying when the trend is going down, reflecting a counter-trend strategy.

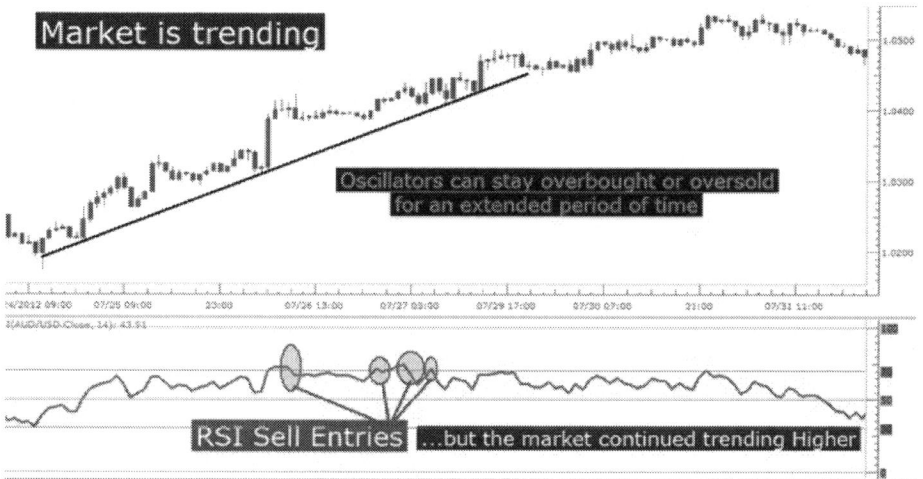

In this second chart, the price trend was going upwards until 4 different sell triggers occurred. Once the RSI moved below 70, trading losses can occur, that's why the sell or exit signal was placed just before that signal happened. These 4 red dots in the chart presented opportunities to sell.

Entry: Entering on an overbought or oversold signal will require you to buy to or sell as soon as the price action goes out of the threshold shown on the RSI indicator. If you choose to trade in a divergence with the help of the RSI indicator, it is best to enter in the direction of the said indicator, preferably after 2-3 candles in a row after the price action closes.

Exit: The optimal place for your stop loss order is beyond a swing at the top or bottom, created at the time of the reversal you will be trading. Remember this: hold your trade until there appears an opposite signal coming from the RSI indicator. Practically speaking, only take out your profits by using price action rules; otherwise, a pre-determined stop loss can secure your gains.

Chapter 4 - Secrets to Becoming a Successful Forex Trader

There is truly not one recipe for success in any kind of job or industry, but there are a few consistent traits that one must have in order to be a successful Forex trader. By this time, you would have already understood what the Forex is all about, and you even have determined your trading strategy. But knowing what works for you is just the tip of the iceberg. Having a specific set of traits can help spell the difference between a successful trader from an unsuccessful one.

Characteristics of Successful Investors and Traders

The best traders are those who are able to master their emotions and can keep them fully controlled. They are aware that they are in control of the destiny of their long-term investment strategy and management of their portfolio. Below are some of the traits they possess and are a must in your personality as soon as you decide to go trading and consistently make money.

They are a risk and money manager first, and as an investor and trader second. This means that even successful investors and traders know exactly that adopting a rule-based money management strategy is one of the more critical concepts of risk management. They know that they need skills in investing and trading, but an understanding and mastery of being a money and risk manager comes first. This is what makes them consistently profitable investors and traders.

They know that from the moment they enter a trade, their money is exposed to the live market. The only thing to control by then is how much money you don't lose. To be consistently profitable, know that the profits will take care of themselves if you consistently implement sound money management practices while your money is in the live market. Instead of thinking about how much money you will make, think about what is the maximum amount of money they do not want to lose on any one particular position. This entails employing a rule-based method of using a stop loss and sometimes exiting a position before their stop loss is triggered, once they feel their analysis was in error. Being able to re-assess every now and then and determining when to exit is an advantage they have above other traders.

They know when to enter a trade. Experienced and successful traders look for set-ups, which offer a low-risk, high-reward outcome with the highest probability of success for them. They see to it that they enter a trade with a stop loss that is as close to their entry as possible, in order to have the lowest amount of risk involved. This still reflects their great risk management skills, as previously mentioned. Apart from knowing what their profit margin is, they also take into consideration their margin of error before taking a position.

They know that losses are part of doing business, as well as learning. Because of this, a great trader knows how to turn a negative into a positive. It is well known that trading is a risk-taking business, and if you are not prepared to take on a certain amount of risk, then gaining rewards might not be for you. You must be able to master your own psychology and have a thorough command of your emotions. Most of all, learn to be comfortable about taking losses. It will happen, and the best thing you can do is minimise it, and make a positive reaction out of it. Do not dwell on what could have, or what should have been.

They know how to overcome fear and greed. These are two things that are very common in traders. It leads traders not to know when to let go of a position when it is moving against them. Instead, learn to quantify and monetise fear. Figure out how much your position goes against you, and that in turn will help you see the fact in the light. Greed is easily overcome by having with you a rule-based plan that tells you your strategy. When one works according to the plan set up, there is no room for greed because everything you are doing is already predetermined.

They are knowledgeable. The more you know about the assets you are working with, the better. As part of your operating plan, you must do your research and educate yourself on these assets. This can also help minimise fear when trading, as confidence takes its place instead. Know what you are doing, and why. Get the right information because, with it, you will be able to make the type of high-level decisions needed to make money in the live markets.

They stick to their rule-based plan. In fact, having a simple plan is the only way to have a profitable significant edge in the live markets. It doesn't have to be complicated in order for it to be successful. While different traders have different rules for different methods, allowing the plan to be implemented and letting the rules do the work ensures them a successful trading most of the time. With strict adherence to their own rule-based plan, they are confident and without fear when going into the live market. It gives them the best opportunity for a highly probable positive outcome and long-term survival in the live markets.

They have realistic expectations. A lot of new traders and coming into this business have unrealistic expectations from the very start. They tend to focus too much on making money, basing their decisions on how much they are going to make as opposed to how much money they can lose. This false sense of success can be a huge letdown once they start to lose right away. Remember this: while you can certainly make a lot of money in the Forex market, it will most likely not happen as fast as you think.

Chapter 5 - Glossary of Terms

Account Margin – The percentage or deposit to which your leverage will be applied to when you trade.

Bid price – The price at which you can sell a currency.

Candlesticks – A type of chart that displays the high, low, open, and closing prices of a security for a specific period

Leverage – The instrument that allows a trader to borrow and control much larger amounts of collateral, by using relatively small personal investment. This means that profits can be made from relatively small currency price movements. While it will increase the value of any profits, it can also rapidly multiply any losses.

Limit-entry order – An instruction to buy at a certain level below the current market price, or an instruction to sell at a certain level above the current market price.

Long position/Going long – When a trade is based on a transaction where the trader is predicting that the price of a currency will increase over the duration.

Lots – Structure the specific amounts that can be applied to each trade.

Margin – The amount of money that you will need to personally put towards a trading transaction.

Market Order/Unrestricted Order – An instruction to buy or sell at the best available price.

Offer/Ask – The price you will be quoted when you wish to buy currency.

Pip – The change in value between two currencies. For example, when the value of USD/GBP moves from 1.5015 to 1.5016, that movement is counted as one pip.

Short position/Going short - When a trade is based on a transaction where the trader is predicting that the price of a currency will decrease over the duration.

Spread – The difference between the bid and offer price.

Stop Order – An instruction to buy or sell when the price reaches a predetermined level, for the purposes of limiting potential losses or locking in profitable gains.

Taking a position – A term used to describe when a trade is being made.

Trailing stop – A specific type of stop order that moves in relation to fluctuations in price.

Conclusion

The reality of Forex trading is that it becomes competitions at the highest level, where stakes are piled high. The most important thing for you as a beginner is to educate yourself to be a competitor and as a winner. Be prepared to work with the best market participants in the world, and try not to get killed!

Also, do not enter the live market with real money until you are ready. This only causes you to lose all of that and question your skills. Instead, start off slow and build on success. Study each and every aspect of all the resources you can have your hands on. This will take as long as it needs to, but there is no need to hurry because the market will always be there waiting for you.

Most of all, have structure and discipline. Without these, it will be hard to become consistently profitable in the future. Take your time in being organised about your every move. This way, you can develop your training edge and have it mastered by the time you enter the live trade. It takes a lot of time and patience, but with determination, you will eventually pull through.

I wish you all the best as you start your journey towards being a Forex trader. Happy investing!

-- **Leigh Vernon**

Printed in Great Britain
by Amazon